So Kind Yet So Cruel

So Kind Yet So Cruel

The Reawakening of Peoplehood

FUMITAKA MATSUOKA

CASCADE *Books* • Eugene, Oregon

SO KIND YET SO CRUEL
The Reawakening of Peoplehood

Cascade Books
An Imprint of Wipf and Stock Publishers
199 W. 8th Ave., Suite 3
Eugene, OR 97401

www.wipfandstock.com

PAPERBACK ISBN: 979-8-3852-2621-4
HARDCOVER ISBN: 979-8-3852-2622-1
EBOOK ISBN: 979-8-3852-2623-8

Cataloguing-in-Publication data:

Names: Matsuoka, Fumitaka, author.

Title: So kind yet so cruel : the reawakening of Peoplehood / Fumitaka Matsuoka.

Description: Eugene, OR: Cascade Books, 2026. | Includes bibliographical references.

Identifiers: ISBN 979-8-3852-2621-4 (paperback) | ISBN 979-8-3852-2622-1(hardcover) | ISBN 979-8-3852-2623-8 (ebook)

Subjects: LCSH: National characteristics, America. | Minorities—United States. | Ethnicity—United States. | United States—Race relations.

Classification: E169.12 M3755 2026 (paperback) | E169.12 (ebook)

03/05/26

This book is dedicated to Sharon G. Thornton. Without her generous conversations and insightful suggestions this book would not have been given its birth. This is the labor of her love.

Contents

Preface

THE QUESTION I ASK in this book is this: What makes Americans American? It can be said that the conventional answer to this question is "Out of Many, One." We can pretty much agree upon the meaning of "Out of Many." But how about "One"? I am not sure if we have a commonly agreed upon answer to the meaning of "One," particularly in this age of polarization. Polarization is also a word popularly used to suggest sharply drawn divisions and boundary-creating among people, groups, or individuals. And yet, polarization is the word to describe the quality of relationships, how we relate with each other. More precisely, it points to the oppositional character of the way we relate with each other and the divisions or brokenness we witness in society today. In our hyper-individualized society, we would like to assume that the divisions we witness are the disconnections and separations as a result of being autonomous individuals. But they tell us something else. They are in fact, an indication of a particular way of relating with each other that I will call "meeting as strangers" and not as neighbors. As strangers we do not attempt to create a common story of our shared life together. Our polarization reveals more of who and what we each are, a people who oppose each other rather than people seeking authentic relationships with each other.

In more relationally oriented societies polarization can be viewed as an indicator of the unhealth of the entire society rather than the self-contained expressions of each person or a group of people. In the words of Norwegian singer-songwriter Sigrid, the polarization we experience is people surrounding themselves with "Strangers, perfect *pretenders*." "We're falling head over heels, For something that ain't real. It could never be us, eh Just you and I."[1] I realize that this may well be an overstatement of the current state of polarization. But I ask, do we really know each other, the strangers we meet, even our friends? Do we really care for each other? Perhaps some

1. Sigrid, "Strangers."

do, but there is a large group of people who do not, particularly when it comes to race relations. We tend to be "Strangers, perfect *pretenders*."

Contradictions, neglect, apathy, and distrust in relating with people have long been the experiences of those of us who are people of color as we relate with majority-race people. Filipino poet Carlos Bulosan put the oppositional and contradictory manner of relationships of Americans this way: "Why are Americans so kind and yet so cruel?" Many of us still ask this question as we ponder the meaning of what it means to live in this land together. We used to think that the kindness we saw in *Father Knows Best* spoke to us all. But we knew deep down that there were people for whom kindness was just one side of being Americans. There is another side, cruelty, that has been a daily occurrence for many. Public lynching and sending people to concentration camps because of the rumors of espionage and subversion may not be so blatant today as they were in our past. But violence is still rampant and cruel today, often publicly sanctioned as in the way we treat undocumented people. Pushing people away is such a violent act. Homelessness and the border crisis are stubborn and brutal, making the gap between the privileged and the deprived, a constant reminder that there is a hollowness in the words of those who have taken pride in upholding life, liberty, and the pursuit of happiness. Why have we been so kind to some and so cruel to others? Why are we eager to hear the life stories of friends and so indifferent to hear the stories of strangers, particularly racialized strangers? This is the question facing our peoplehood.

"Why are Americans so kind and yet so cruel?" Bulosan's question is as critical today as when he asked it seventy-eight years ago.[2] What frame of reference can we reliably employ to address this question? I would like to bring faith to the forefront for engaging this pivotal question. By faith I mean "the trusted stories of people" who have experienced what Bulosan is pointing to in his question. These stories reveal the presence of contradictions, "kindness and cruelty," in our history and our present time. I realize that faith is not generally viewed as a suitable means to talk about the subject of peoplehood, a subject we more likely assume to belong in the realm of "reasoned knowledge" of political and social sciences. What is at stake in the question of kindness and cruelty may be seen as that which needs to be addressed through an analysis of the systems of governance and power, where decision-making is a subject matter of who receives what and how through the structures of governance. We are inclined to seek to

2. Bulosan, *America Is in the Heart*, 160.

"understand" human patterns that enable us to analyze how our institutions interact. Social analysis is necessary and valuable, and it can make introducing faith seem overly tame, docile, and too private, the wrong framework to address the complex subject of race relations as they pertain to our history of what it means to be American. But our peoplehood began in the context of faith.

Puritanism and Pietism were the powerful foundations of our nation. The rise of individualism also had deep roots in the soul of America as it influenced understandings of liberty, equality, and justice. The subject of who and what we are, the questions about our quality of life, and the depth meaning of our life and what we trust, are not merely that of rational knowledge and understanding. Questions of meaning and trust involve more than head knowledge. We have overly relied upon social sciences alone to address the subject that really belongs to the realm of a lived faith that speaks to our hearts. A social scientific approach has its place in treating the subject of contradictions involved in race relationships. It helps us grasp how we tend to behave within the world we created throughout our history—the patterns of relationships we have established in creating and governing our societies. We also need to realize that social scientific approaches to the question of peoplehood are deeply grounded in the ways people see themselves impacted by the religious, philosophical, and cultural assumptions, and racialized interpretation of these during any given age. "Understanding"—in this instance social science understanding—is not universally applicable to all inquiries. Parker Palmer reminds us:

> We must judge ourselves by a higher standard than effectiveness, the standard called faithfulness. Are we faithful to the community on which we depend, to doing what we [can do] in response to its pressing needs? Are we faithful to the better angels of our nature and to what they call forth from us? Are we faithful to the eternal conversation of the human race, to speaking and listening in a way that takes us closer to truth? Are we faithful to the call of courage that summons us to witness to the common good, even against great odds? When faithfulness is our standard, we are more likely to sustain our engagement with tasks that will never end; doing justice, loving mercy, and calling the beloved community into being.[3]

3. Palmer, *Healing the Heart of Democracy*, 193.

This confessional framework of Christian faith, which is the orientation of this work, involves the trusted stories and experience of all our people. To be sure, it is not only embodied in idealized, politicized, racialized popular expressions of a particular religious community. It is equally the wisdom that has spoken to a variety of American people in history. And it is a wisdom that continues to speak to many of our hearts today, even in this time of religious and other forms of pluralism. Faith during the founding of this country, was explicitly Puritan and Pietistic Christianity in orientation. It eventually took numerous diverse expressions. But faith, particularly the uncritical assumptions that accompanied its incorporation into our founding documents and ways of life, has been plagued by contradictions. This faith orientation has never been universal. Frederick Douglass spoke of the hollowness of a faith that sanctioned the suffering of African American people when he powerfully named the Fourth of July as the Day to Mourn, not the day to celebrate. Faith as an orienting factor can be used for ill. Frederick Douglass shows how it impacted and harmed his and others' lives. At the same time, the life story of John Lewis, whom we will consider in the first chapter, reveals how faith can also be a powerful motivation for good. For good or ill, better or worse, faith has played a significant role in our American story. While it is deeply personal and confessional, it is also communal and public and plays an important part in understanding who we are and where we have come from.

Trusted stories, viewed using a faith perspective, give us ways to address the questions we ask about ourselves, our limitations and potentials, about our pain and joy of life, what we trust, and what are our sources of courage and hope. They also give us motivation and encouragement on how to relate to our neighbors. Faith needs to be reclaimed for its original role, the role of not knowing precisely what is happening in us, or precisely where we are going. Faith is woven into the public life of our history. It is part of our public life of being an American as it is deeply personal. As embedded in our foundation, it has created the ways we relate with each other and the ways we continue to try to live together. We need to pay attention to the role of faith in order to address our challenges and possibilities. The faith framework of this book is a trustworthy approach to address the question: Why is America so kind and yet so cruel?

Humility will be needed to enter into the framework of trusted stories and experiences. The kind of humility I am talking about is an aspect of a faith orientation. By this I mean that humility relies less on causal reasoning and more on open inquiry—curiosity, if you will. We need to admit that "we really don't know what we don't know" as my colleague Professor Archie Smith Jr. would put it. We need to have an openness to something more than ourselves and our familiar perspectives. We need to be curious about something that touches us even if we cannot identify with its source. Too often when we do not "understand" someone, or when we fail to naturally relate to their unfamiliar experience, we become defensive, dismissive, and frequently lacking in compassion. In other words, cruel. The question, why are we so kind and yet so cruel is the challenge of people connected and disconnected, the question of human relatedness, which is the question of faith. Cruelty really involves the tragic absence of the neglected stories of our communal life. Without hearing the voices of the neglected, the story of our peoplehood, our shared life becomes tragic and untrustworthy. What will be proposed in this work is that for our life to become trustworthy and credible to all people we will need to acknowledge and accept our contradictory history. And this will take humility.

My point in this book is that we Americans are relationally broken. We have treated our neighbors more as strangers than friends. The weight of the words, "Life, liberty, and the pursuit of happiness" can still speak to our individual and communal hearts when we admit the brokenness of our life together. As we move through this work, I will point out that ever so slowly we are beginning to see ourselves differently both personally and in our life together. In the midst of the our broken relationships, why Americans are so kind yet so cruel is starting to reveal different levels of meaning implied in that question. This awareness of our brokenness reveals a surprising faith and an unspoken trust in the web that holds us even in the midst of our brokenness.

Martin Luther King Jr. speaks to our challenge of trying to make a true peoplehood, especially given our history of painful race relations: "People fail to get along because they fear each other; they fear each other because they don't know each other; they don't know each other because they have not communicated with each other." In other words, our relationships are broken. Pastoral theologian Archie Smith Jr. says relationality "is a way of speaking of the indwelling presence of others in our own concrete reality and of our presence in others."[4] For the rebirth of peoplehood, then, we need to listen, hear and trust other people's experiences just as one's own. This is a particular challenge for the majority people. This means that

4. Smith, *Relational Self*, 51.

America can never be a "people" unless we all recognize and acknowledge in our heads and feel in our hearts the lives of people who do not share our own familiar life experiences, particularly racial differences. We are Americans because we share being a people of various life outlooks. The "relational self" says that one's well-being is not attained at the expense of another person's well-being, but that the well-being of others is also our own well-being. I am proposing that the reality of a relational self can help us truly become "We the People."

I am using a historical faith framework of Christian confessional theology to address the polarization and brokenness in our society. I am saying that our polarization and brokenness are more than a social science problem. It is a relational issue. Therefore, I am advocating the recovery of a relationally oriented faith reading of human life, particularly how this addresses race relations in our history. My wish is that this book will help bring about serious conversations at a level where faith perspectives have either been missed or underappreciated in previous conversations on the subject of peoplehood.

Introduction

Let America be America again.
Let it be the dream it used to be.
Let it be the pioneer on the plain
Seeking a home where he himself is free.

(America never was America to me.)

Let America be the dream the dreamers dreamed—
Let it be that great strong land of love
Where never kings connive nor tyrants scheme
That any man be crushed by one above.

(It never was America to me.)

O, let my land be a land where Liberty
Is crowned with no false patriotic wreath,
But opportunity is real, and life is free,
Equality is in the air we breathe.

(There's never been equality for me,
Nor freedom in this "homeland of the free.")

From "Let America Be America Again," by Langston Hughes[1]

1. Hughes, *Collected Poems of Langston Hughes,* 189.

Let America be that great strong land of love. We are a gathering of people who come together without being crushed by one above. This is the way poet Langston Hughes talked about America, by illuminating the African American condition. What it means to be an American has been asked numerous times in a variety of settings throughout our history. The question is taking on an added and fresh significance in this age of hyper-polarization. The question is both current and historical. It asks how we read and understand our national history and how we treat our neighbors given the heightened oppositional fashion we relate with each other. The question of what it means to be American people is the question of how we relate with each other. I employ the term "Peoplehood" to mean the collective sense and character of belonging to a distinct gathering of people and the question of how we relate with each other even though we may see some as familiar neighbors and others as suspicious strangers.

Peoplehood is more than the citizenship that describes our American identity with its status as a separate and independent nation. Peoplehood asks the question of both the meaning of our history and the state of how we relate with each other as a people today. It is also the question sociologist Robert N. Bellah asked in *Habits of the Heart:* What moves us, the beliefs and practices that shape our character and give form to our social order?[2] I maintain that there are also "counter-habits of the heart" amidst the prevailing and familiar habits of the heart, that move some segments of our people.

The counter-habits are often not well noticed and appreciated. These neglected habits belong to the disregarded segments of our peoplehood. The coexistence of the publicly accustomed habits of the heart and the less known counter-habits of the heart constitute who we are as Americans, the people of contradictions. This book probes ways of both the familiar habits and the neglected counter-habits of the heart in order to reveal American peoplehood for what it really is. I treat this vast and complex subject in a limited fashion through the lens of faith. Faith means the "trusted story" of people. To put it another way, this book is confessional and speaks to my own heart. At the same time, while it is my confessional work, it also relates to a wider community and has historical resonances. This book is not predominantly an analytical endeavor though the resources I employ for treating the central questions of the contradictory character of peoplehood are epistemologically inclusive.

2. Bellah et al., *Habits of the Heart*, cover copy.

The question of what it means to be an American, as I say, is a highly personal one for me. As a transnational person, born, raised, and educated in Japan for some twenty years and having spent considerably more years in the US as a citizen, I believe I have a distinct perspective on American peoplehood. America is both a foreign land for me and "home." American peoplehood cannot be bifurcated. America is one as well as the other. This perspective is the basis for the way I view America as a people of contradictions, both historically and relationally today. We say we are "Out of Many, One." We believe this is what unites us through a celebration of our differences. But I say that we are not really one. Yes, we are many, but not one. I believe "Out of Many, We" is a more accurate way of describing our peoplehood. I say so because we have no difficulty saying yes to the words, "Out of many," but can we say together the word "One" and mean it? Yes, we are Americans. But our meanings of what America means are often so different. "One" is not the reality of our peoplehood. Rather, we collectively yearn for what we can be together even as strangers and as familiar neighbors.

I have noticed that my view of America is not so peculiar to my own life formation. I have discovered similar views and interpretations of American peoplehood among American-born scholars and intellectuals as well. "A Nation of Contradictions" is the term used by scholars such as Rodney Clapp, Rodney E. Slater and journalists Andrew Sullivan, Emily St. James, and numerous others who speak of a similar impression of who we are as people.[3] Slater reminds us that Frederick Douglass in his day posed the famous question, "What to the Slave is the Fourth of July?" And then he claimed that "This Fourth (of) July is yours, not mine. You may rejoice, I must mourn." Filipino poet Carlos Bulosan in a similar fashion asks, "Why are Americans so kind and so cruel?" These are also questions I pose in this book. I contend that the polarization we witness today stems from the very history and practice of our contradictory way of living together. We relate with each other oppositionally. We have difficulty complementing each other.

What drives the peoplehood of contradictions? I maintain that we have a very positivistic image of ourselves, both in public and in private. We have an aversion to hearing the stories of sufferings, chaos, and negation amongst us. For example, historian Philip Gleason comments on this in his "American Identity and Americanization":

3. Slater, "July Fourth."

> To be or to become an American, a person did not have to be any particular national, linguistic, religious, or ethnic background. And all he [*sic*] had to do was to commit himself to the political ideology centered on the abstract ideals of liberty, equality, and republicanism. Thus, the universalist ideological character of American nationality meant that it was open to anyone who willed to become an American.[4]

In other words, to become American one must agree to ignore a certain price in doing so. The price is silencing one's own experiences of suffering, anguish, and chaos in life in order to "fit in" to a taken-for-granted liberty and equality for all.

America is ideologically built and sustained on the societal values of liberty, equality, and the representative form of republicanism as these values are celebrated on the Fourth of July. This is the public face of American people. Theologian Douglas John Hall names this positivism of North America by calling us "an officially optimistic society."[5]

Optimism derives from the belief that history is redemptive, that the golden age is before us and not behind us. We believe in progress if we work hard enough for it. Combined with the doctrine of progress is the doctrine of work: "it is for us to clear the path." This optimism has become the dominant force behind our prevailing habits of the heart.[6] Reinhold Niebuhr reminds us that "the dominant note in modern culture is not so much confidence in reason as faith in history. The conception of redemptive history informs the most diverse forms of modern culture."[7]

But the question about our confidence for the future, i.e., optimism, raises the question about how we approach the abyss we encounter and experience. How does optimism address unjust sufferings, catastrophes, disintegrations, and chaos that inevitably come to us? Do our familiar habits of the heart, with our confidence in redemptive history, prepare us for experiences of negation? This is the question that runs through the lives of the neglected people of contradictions. Without acknowledging and addressing the dimension of the void in our lives, the depth meaning of the soul of America, equality, liberty, and justice, cannot be truly revealed, understood, and owned by "we the people." Reinhold Niebuhr calls faith

4. Gleason, *American Identity and Americanization*, 31–32.

5. Hall, *Lighten Our Darkness*, 43–59.

6. Hall, *Lighten Our Darkness*, 54.

7. Niebuhr, *Faith and History*, 3.

in history "the acceptance of the abyss we experience without being overwhelmed by it."[8] This is the true meaning of what is revealed in our history and the present state of peoplehood. Optimism and negation exist together in our peoplehood, informing each other. But the weight of these contradictions rests on the side of optimism and not acknowledging and accepting the presence of negation in our history and experiences.

In order to explore the revelatory meaning of contradictions I employ a particular method of exploration. I address the conflicted history and present status of peoplehood through the perspective of what H. Richard Niebuhr calls "an internal history" rather than "external history."[9] That is, I focus on the "memory of the heart" and "the memory that is lived" and not an external reading of the memory "as seen." The "memory of the heart" that speaks deep into our being functions to "illuminate" and make "intelligible" the painful as well as the positivistic side of our collective belief and history. "Revelation" in my work means the revelatory character of American peoplehood in history, past and present. What is revealed about our peoplehood in history is both optimism and void. The question I ask is this: What is the impact and implications of the "memory of the heart," and the history as lived, that still continues to live today to shape who we are? We have not paid much attention to the history of void and negation of life.

Our future is not completely unknown. Our experiences of today point toward a future that has been introduced in the past. Our memories live both in the habits and counter-habits of the heart, habits that make the familiar common habits of the heart truly intelligible by revealing their origin, history, limitations, and how they are practiced today. In other words, the understanding and acknowledgment of the history and practices of the neglected side of our peoplehood will reveal our historically rooted contradictions and how they are still lived today. This, I contend, will help deepen the meaning of our publicly stated "self-evident truths" of equality, freedom, and justice.

The peoplehood of contradictions points to how we related with our neighbors in the past and how we continue to relate to them today. The unacknowledged contradictions mean we approach our "unknown" and "unseen" neighbors basically as strangers, not as friends. The truth that binds us together is a paradox. We are bound together while in another sense we are alone and isolated. To know this is to know that deep in us

8. See Niebuhr, *Faith and History*, 55–69.

9. See Niebuhr, *Meaning of Revelation*, 44–66.

we need each other when we meet neighbors as well as strangers. As writer Frederick Buechner says, "more than most time we dare to admit."[10] Only when we internalize the neglected "other side" of our history can the full meaning of our founding words, that make up the "Soul of America," enter into our public heart as a shared vision of who we can be. We need to meet and treat strangers as neighbors.

The question of what it means to be an American, individually and as a people, is a highly personal one for me. As mentioned earlier, I am a trans-local person, born, raised, and educated in Japan for some twenty years, and now living the remainder of my life in the United States as a US citizen. I came as a student and recently retired from an academic life of teaching, writing, and administration in theological institutions. I believe I have a distinct perspective on American peoplehood. America is both a foreign land to me and "home." American peoplehood is one as well as the other. This perspective is the way I view America, as a people of contradictions both historically and relationally today. The central question I pose in this work is the question Carlos Bulosan asked: "Why are Americans so kind and yet so cruel?" The question wells up out of my personal life as well. But the question also flows out of a communal life of the neglected people. "Benign neglect," at best, seems to be the norm for the way a large segment of Americans is treated.

I am conscious of the dearth of works on the subject of peoplehood and race from the vantage point of the Americans of Asian descent, Asian American and Pacific Islanders communities (AAPI). While not developing this theme to the extent that it deserves, I am introducing this particular group of Americans to speak of their side of the contradictions. The often-assumed voices of people of color tend to be largely that of African Americans. I deeply appreciate their contributions. As a matter of fact, this book originated in the story of the funeral procession of John Lewis that deeply spoke to my heart. At the same time, I have known the black and white dipolar framework of race conversation tends to omit the voices of other people of color, in my case, those of AAPI communities. This is an aspect that needs to be addressed and explored in more depth in the future. In this work I introduce their voices in order to provide a more balanced and nuanced landscape of the race scene as I consider the depth meaning of "Out of Many, We" in our hyperpolarized society today.

The summary of my approach to peoplehood is as follows.

10. Buechner, *Hungering Dark*, 47.

PART ONE: RACE: THE MESSENGER OF TORN PEOPLEHOOD

Chapter One: People of a Torn Fabric

The life of John Lewis exemplifies a distinctive way of belonging to America that is based on experiences of exclusion and struggles toward inclusion. His life exemplifies the people who live the life of contradictions, historically and as amplified in the current polarizations. His life experiences press the question: Can we pass from the chaotic present time of alienated peoplehood still plagued by contradictions to a new age and world where the separate and equal are the endowed reality for all? The answer to this question remains elusive. But as Lewis said: "Never give up. Never give in. Never become hostile . . . Hate is too big burden to bear."[11] His life exemplifies both the habits of the heart and the counter-habits of the broken heart of our peoplehood together.

Chapter Two: History of Contradictions— Never Fully Achieved Yet Never Forgotten

Here I examine the origin and the meaning of the publicly stated soul of America: the "One" that arises out of many (*e pluribus Unum*), the original glue that was designed to hold people together that claimed "self-evident truths" of equality, freedom, and justice in the form of republicanism. This statement raises the question of how we approach and read the meaning of US history. The message of "Out of Many, One" was meant to be the positivistic "celebration" of diversity (Philip Gleason). I maintain this original proclamation has been experienced by historically unacknowledged people as the foundation for the "contradictions of a nation." The contradictions speak about those who are confident in what has been stated officially on the one hand, and on the other hand those who cannot trust those declarations outright because of their life experiences that say, "not optimistic." Contradictions are not merely differences in perspectives. They go to the very heart of what it means to be a people. "I would submit that a nation cannot restore what it has not established," as civil rights leader Benjamin E. May has said. "The nation exempted blacks and, to a large degree, native Americans from

11. Spoken by Lewis at the August 28, 1963 March on Washington, DC for jobs and freedom.

the dialectics of freedom."[12] How can we talk about being a people when we exclude some for the sake of privileging others?

I will continue to emphasize that we need to hear and own the inconvenient truths in the voices of the voiceless if we want our quest for "We the People" to become honest, authentic, and compelling. Then the words of our founding documents might become our consented words for all when the unappreciated, nonprivileged people truly become "us."

The task before us is learning a new language of peoplehood that honors the deep meaning of the "other side of our history" in this country. True American peoplehood can arise out of our collective yearning and need of each other. An appreciation of the traditional soul of America—equality, freedom, and justice—will depend on acknowledging and embracing the neglected stories of our society. Reweaving the tattered fabric begins with an acknowledgment of the contradictions and what they mean for a nation polarized and at odds with itself. We are a "separate and unequal" people today. Where do we go from here?

PART TWO: THE COUNTER-HABITS OF THE HEART

Chapter Three: Nonsingular Consciousness

How can we grow our national and communal heart to know and appreciate the counter-habits of the heart? How can we "feel" the pain and sufferings of people whose distinctive ways of belonging to America is based on experiences of exclusion and struggles toward inclusion? Nurturing different ways of knowing is needed in order for the whole peoplehood to become owned by us. To this end, there is a growing awareness of nurturing nonsingular consciousness, or "double consciousness" (W. E. B. DuBois) and even multiple consciousness. This growing awareness means not only knowing the "other," but also a critical way to know more of one's own self. Nonsingular consciousness is a powerful way of living with our historical contradictions in order to discern the deeper meanings of race and how the multiple meanings impact our life together. DuBois's "double consciousness" is a given in the lives of people of color, even though we embrace it imperfectly. It is a way of self-representation even amidst the pressures to see ourselves through the eyes of the majority people.

12. Van Allen, ed., *American Religious Values and the Future of America*, 17.

For the racially dominant people, nurturing nonsingular consciousness is needed for relationship-building in order to rediscover the intricate web of our humanity. But it is exceedingly difficult because to nurture a multiple consciousness for this group of people is an act of choice. It does not come naturally even while it needs to become necessary in order to reach out to others who are unfamiliar. To intentionally adopt a nonsingular consciousness means not reaching out to unfamiliar neighbors from the position of sufficiency, strength, and power, but out of a need to live the truth that our lives are all linked together in a shared web of relationships.

Chapter Four: Defiant Hope

Are we willing to value a different kind of hope? Are we willing to enter into a "defiant hope," different from the familiar aspirational hope, as we face increasing fragmentation and polarization? In the spirit of John Lewis, to embrace defiant hope together is to refuse the despairing belief that history is only a chaos of rival forces.

A critical contradiction in the understanding of peoplehood is the word "hope." The preamble of the US Constitution is an aspirational statement. "We the People of the United States, *in order to form a more perfect union* . . ." For people of neglected voices, equality, freedom, and justice are more than aspirational words. These words speak of defiant hope, hope against hope, that arises out of their experiences of pain, sufferings, and hopelessness. "Never give up. Never give in. Never become hostile . . . Hate is too big a burden to bear," says John Lewis. Hope against hope, or defiant hope, comes in spite of the seemingly hopeless situation a people may be facing. It means continuing to hope in spite of overwhelming odds. Defiant hope drives us to maintain our determination amidst the forces that extinguish hope.

Chapter Five: The Illusion of Precision

The future of race is the emergence of a nomadic way of life that shifts away from the familiar and inflexible racial demarcations and identities we have caged ourselves in. In the place of fixed ways of portraying us, racial identities are dynamic and spirited. So is the meaning of peoplehood. We have lived in the midst of an "illusion of precision" for so long in the race landscape. While the historically rigid classifications of racial groups still continue and speak deeply to the pain and identity of people of color, racial differences are becoming less precise, shifting the ways we frame the question of race. "Disruption of preconceived expectations" is how sociologists Michael Omi and Howard Winant characterize this emerging understanding of race that is taking place.[13] The question before us is whether Americans can embrace this changing reality of selfhood and our emerging "disorienting self."[14]

One way of understanding this process of shifting identities for racial communities is hybridization. Hybridization of race is not simply moving between racial identities. It has more to do with how immigrant communities deal with the contradicitions and violence of the United States. The illusion of precision in race points beyond the fluidity of racial identities to a different quality of life where a shift from a stable meaning of life moves toward an awareness of a nomadic and unsettled way of life. "It is the morality of not being at home in one's own home" (Theodore Adorno). It is the "rough first draft" of the reweaving of peoplehood.

Conclusion: Joining Trusted Stories

When life is unstable, relationships can become valued. The question is how will this "non master's tool," as Audrey Lorde characterizes the new paradigm,[15] live side by side with the precise and contradictory ways of living and relating with each other? The challenge before us, as we look toward the future of a people "becoming and belonging," is that of being honest about our history of contradictions from which we have become who we are today—strangers to each other. I explore the notion of solidarity with our "neighbors becoming friends" through the learning of a new language and understanding its new meaning. We continue to live with discontent among us, an unease that in part arises from our shifting identities, especially when it involves race. I believe as we strive, not for a "more perfect union," rather an honest union, our future will rest on the cultivation of a new sense of solidarity with our neighbors. A new sense of solidarity that binds us together through our shared pain in recognizing the contradictions we have inherited and live with today. As we together learn

13. Omi and Winant, *Racial Formation in the United States*, 59.

14. Busto, *Revealing the Sacred*, 9.

15. See Lorde, *Sister Outsider*, 110.

a new language to communicate with each other, we will reweave the torn fabric of our relationships.

"Why are Americans so kind and yet so cruel?" In many ways I have posed this question over and over again in my experience of being an outsider and then becoming an insider of American peoplehood. This is the question I have posed in this work. Some of my kind friends who were generous and good-hearted turned out to have no inkling or understanding of who I am and what I cherish. My neighbors turned out to be strangers, both kind and cruel in the same person. This society values the aspirations of each member while it neglects the hardships of too many of its members.

In my research into writing this work I learned that "Why are Americans so kind and so cruel?" is a common question many people of color ask. John Lewis witnessed this question in his own life in his struggle with racism and his representation in Congress. Throughout his life, he continued to believe and practice what America is all about—equality, freedom, and justice. He gave himself to public service. And, he practiced defiance, "good trouble"—not resignation or defeat. The public side of our peoplehood needs to listen deeply to Lewis and others who have been treated as strangers for so long and yet continued to believe in the peoplehood of this land. Like Lewis, there are others of us who once we know we have been strangers in a broken web of people, we hope against hope that more of us will long for a mended web where we can treat all strangers as neighbors. We need each other not as opponents, but as friends. This is a simple but profound lesson for our peoplehood.

This book approaches American peoplehood from a neglected and overlooked angle of reading history. It is a perspective of history that reveals the presence of the counter-habits of our collective heart, the habits that well up from our deep internal memory, not from the individualistic or external memory of facts written in a document. What is revealed in this version of our history is the deep contradictions of our habits that have run through our collective lives all along—the contradictions of celebration and mourning, kindness and cruelty, optimism and defiance, and desire for stability and intimacy in the midst of a nomadic life. One might argue that the voices of the voiceless are available everywhere. The question is whether we can really hear them in our hearts.

The life of contradictions has brought us to today's polarized, adversarial, and mutually alienated relationships because hearing the voices are so difficult and daunting. Anthropologist Ruth Behar says that all we can do is to "translate" them, and not "represent" them.[16] Reawakening of peoplehood begins with admitting the trusted counter-stories of people, likely the story of strangers, that will bring us to a deeper appreciation and commitment to a public story of the whole people. Solidarity with strangers in the midst of contradictions may move us into a more complementary manner of living together in the future.

16. Behar, *Translated Women*. To "translate" and to "represent" are two main concepts of Behar's book.

PART ONE

Race: The Messenger of Torn Peoplehood

In Part One I explore some the background of our society that has given rise to the polarizations we are experiencing today. We are a society torn apart by conflicting experiences, even divergent understandings of our founding documents. This means we have lived with historical contradictions that have become embedded in our experiences of life together today. The contradictions that we live with have deepened our divisions today to the point where we have come to see others as strangers, not as neighbors. Furthermore, these contradictions have magnified the oppositional patterns of race relations over time.

I explore how these contradictions have magnified what has become the oppositional way we treat each other. In fact, these oppositional ways have become the prevailing pattern of our relationships. The contradictions that have solidified into oppositional ways of relating are what I call the brokenness of peoplehood. Our brokenness, not "oneness" is the beginning point of our society. The acknowledgment of the brokenness of our peoplehood is the fundamental framework needed to live into the promises of life, liberty, and the pursuit of happiness. This is an alternative outlook that challenges the taken for granted, and widespread outlook of optimism.

CHAPTER ONE

People of a Torn Fabric

THE SOUL OF AMERICA REVISITED

AMONG THE RECENT PACKED news was a little noticed piece that said that a statue of the late Representative John Lewis was erected in his congressional district in Georgia where a confederate monument once stood. The sculptor of the statue is Basil Watson. His approach to sculpture is this: "I am inspired by the heroic in mankind [*sic*], and am moved to express the vitality, beauty, grace, and strength of the human figure in its varied shapes, sizes, abilities, and functions. The spirit that motivates it is limitless in grandeur."[1] Watson insisted: "The John Lewis story is a powerful story that needs to be told."[2] Indeed the story of Lewis needs to be told because it is a story of America, like many other stories in history that "express the vitality, beauty, grace and strength of the human figure." But vitality, beauty, grace and strength can come with a tremendous cost of disappointment, ugliness, disapproval, and exhaustion. The stories of the cost are abundant among "we the people" but we don't want to hear them. Yet, these stories are deeply lodged in the memories of many of us and motivate us to mold a more trusted story for "We the People." And still, Lewis's love story has been neglected and even erased from our collective memories as we proudly tell the story of the "Truths" that we are endowed with, the "unalienable Rights of Life, Liberty, and the Pursuit of Happiness." At the same time, we know that deep down in our hearts, as historian Jon Meacham reminded us, "We've

1. Seiler, "Atlanta Artist Selected." See also Sayers, "Statue of Late Civil Rights Icon."
2. Seiler, "Atlanta Artist Selected."

always lived with—and perpetuated—fundamental contradictions."[3] The contradictions are that "while whites built and dreamed, people of color were subjugated and exploited by a rising nation that prided itself on the expansion of liberty."[4] Frederick Douglass was more forceful in his day:

> [Y]our boasted liberty, an unholy license; your national greatness, swelling vanity; your sounds of rejoicing are empty and heartless; your denunciations of tyrants, brass fronted impudence; your shouts of liberty and equality, hollow mockery; your prayers and hymns, your sermons and thanksgivings, with all your religious parade, and solemnity, are, to him [the slave], mere bombast, fraud, deception, impiety, and hypocrisy—a thin veil to cover up crimes which would disgrace a nation of savages.[5]

John Lewis's story needs to be told because it reveals that American peoplehood is built upon the two contrasting strands of narrative existing side by side in history: kindness and cruelty, liberty and bondage, and optimism and hope against hope. But we have mostly heard one side to the neglect of the other. Lewis's story needs to be heard so we can make it our own story because our peoplehood is not complete without it.

Our task is not complete. We need to pursue the question: Why do we have an aversion to hear the stories of cruelty, the stories that often arise from people of color and those seen as "different" from the public norms? The not-so-self-evident truth is that our peoplehood has arisen out of both the common aspirational hope for equality, freedom, and justice, as well as out of the stories of those who have not benefited from these sacred words. The reason for hearing one-sided stories lies in what we value. What has been valued and taken for granted in our history is what theologian Douglas John Hall calls our "official optimism."[6] Novelist Sinclair Lewis once said, "Intellectually I know America is no better than any other country; emotionally I know she is better than every other country."[7] Deep down in our hearts many Americans think we know we are exceptional and full of promise. Yet an awful truth is this: "We the People" includes the recognition

3. Meacham, *Soul of America*, 23. The original comment on the nation of contradictions was made by Frederick Douglass's famous words, "What to the Slave Is the Fourth of July?," a speech delivered on July 5, 1852.

4. Meacham, *Soul of America*, 24.

5. Douglass, "Oration in Memory of Abraham Lincoln."

6. Hall, *Lighten Our Darkness*, 43.

7. Meacham, *Soul of America*, 10.

that we are both no better than others even though we desire to "form a more perfect Union." In the midst of the public life full of aspiring hope and optimism we also possess the stories of defiant hope. Amidst a history of unspeakable brutality and hopelessness we hear the stories of hope against hope. John Lewis's story is a story of defiant hope that needs to be told because he truly believed in the people who strive for equality, freedom, and justice. His story is an indispensable and basic building block of who we are. It is a story that has too long been neglected, but also reminds us of the history of those contradictory voices that dwell in our common soul that holds us together. Our peoplehood cannot be built on an optimistic outlook of life alone. Our shared life is built on both optimism and defiance. John Lewis's story needs to be heard so we can be honest about who we are.

History for those who live on the other side of optimism "is more often tragic than comic, full of broken hearts and broken promises, disappointed hopes and dreams delayed."[8] Our soul is rooted in the story of yearning for the reweaving of our broken web of people. Only when more of us own the awful truth of contradictions, intellectually and emotionally, can our creed of life, liberty, and the pursuit of happiness become a genuine and self-evident vision to be strived for as the bond that holds us together. We can be more than the people of contradictions. We can truly become the people who cherish liberty, equality, and justice. John Lewis exemplifies this possibility.

I write this book because America has been to me, as an Asian American, both very kind and yet very cruel, as Filipino poet Carlos Bulosan once noted.[9] I believe we are living out a contradictory history of peoplehood, a history of both kindness and cruelty, equality and bondage, optimism and defiant hope. It is my own life story that also echoes in the lives of many people in this land but has not been readily owned by the wider public. The redemption of our soul of America in the fragmented and polarized life we live begins with owning the history of being the people of contradictions. Facing this history challenges us to face and ask the hard question of why we have such a hard time listening to the life stories of cruelty lived by those who are outside of societal norms. Can we reclaim these stories? What would it take to do so? Our soul, "the air we breathe," as Jon Meacham characterizes it, is that our common vision of the equality of everyone, will become truly compelling when we embrace the life of John Lewis and

8. Meacham, *Soul of America*, 19.

9. Bulosan, *America Is in the Heart*, 160.

others who lived the neglected stories. We will then say to ourselves, "We don't have to be so cruel to each other. We don't have to treat our neighbors as strangers. We cherish equality, liberty, and justice for all." How can we take into our hearts the redeemed soul of our peoplehood? The story of John Lewis, and those who are like him, speak of a new future and invite us to journey toward the redeemed soul. This work joins his quest.

A HIDDEN STORY OF AMERICA

As the nation watched a carriage carrying the body of John Lewis moving slowly across Edmund Pettus Bridge in July 2020, a question arose in my mind: What holds people together in an era of hyperpolarization that alienates one individual from another, one community from another in unparalleled inequality? In that poignant procession of John Lewis's funeral, I also witnessed the beginning of the reawakening of peoplehood, a rebirth so fragile and tenuous that it might not come to fruition, but nevertheless, a rebirth that is defiant, refusing to be cast aside. The declaration of rebirth is not written on a piece of paper, but it is etched in the lives of its founders like the ones who processed across the bridge that day. This declaration is not a one-time event like the one that took place long ago in Independence Hall. Yet, it also began as a movement with founders, named and nameless, rising to a crescendo at a bridge in Alabama where a major founder, John Lewis, was once beaten. The declaration that was enacted in Alabama is the same one that has been declared over and over again throughout our painful history. In the midst of a history that declared the democratic representative form of governance of people, a parallel movement for full participation has also been part of that history. I sense that the declaration of a rebirth of peoplehood will be repeated in the future even if it is neglected and unappreciated, as people reexamine the meaning of the soul of America. The rebirth of this new declaration founded upon telling the contradictory stories of who we have been and who we are today reflects the true soul of America.

What I saw in the procession of John Lewis was a glimpse of the hidden story of America, the story of unspeakable pain and sufferings of voiceless people, the story of their life of anguish and pathos, that is an indispensable building block of our peoplehood that has not been appreciated. The official and popular story of our peoplehood has been that of optimism and progress. We are the people who, "given time and the facts, will make the corrections," as Harry S. Truman once said.[10] We strive together to form a more perfect union, full of confidence and hope. But in the funeral procession of John Lewis, I saw something else that has been hidden in the official story of our people, their sadness of unfulfilled toil and the betrayal of the official promise. What I saw in the procession of John Lewis was the hidden foundation of our peoplehood that has been here all along but has not been appreciated. What I saw in the procession was the story of agony and anguish of people from which a stubborn and defiant hope was born, hope grounded by faith in justice. In the story of John Lewis, a truth about life together has been told amidst the stories of one-sided truths. We are the people of both kindness and cruelty all along, with both aspirational and defiant hope.

And yet, I sensed that something was missing in my impression of the funeral of John Lewis. It took me awhile to name that "something." The question I am asking now: Is the story of John Lewis also my own story? The answer to this question is both yes and no. Yes, his story of a brutal beating by police and his lifelong struggle for civil rights and racial justice very much spoke to me and to my own experience and commitment to the same causes. Lewis indeed represents the conscience of America and has become an icon of our history. His life speaks of what I consider to be the critical challenge facing American people of today and tomorrow. And yet, no matter how exemplary and inspirational John Lewis's life is to me, my own experience of the racial landscape and racial justice is not identical with his experience. The story of his repeated beatings and imprisonment are uniquely his experiences and those of too many African Americans, particularly those of activists. But there are other stories that contribute equally to the awakening of the American soul that have been left behind. One such story is the invisibility and neglect that haunt me and other Americans of Asian descent. The social fabric of America is torn in these ways. The piercing words of scholar of American studies Gary Okihiro point to the intertwining complexity of our web of relationships:

> By seeing only black and white, the presence and absence of all color, whites render Asians, American Indians, and Latinos invisible, ignoring the gradations and complexities of the full spectrum between the racial poles. At the same time, Asians share with Africans the status and repression of nonwhites—as the Other—and therein lies the debilitating aspect

10. Truman quoted by Meacham, *Soul of America*, 255.

> of Asian African antipathy and the liberating nature of African-Asian unity.[11]

American peoplehood is being reborn out of the sufferings of those whose names and life stories have often been ignored and forgotten in the culture of aspirational hope for a perfect union. But even an attempt to acknowledge these voices of pain has been somewhat one-sided. The common unspoken assumption behind an attempt to explore the racial landscape of our people rests upon a black-and-white dyad, as Okihiro points out. The result is that other people of color get left out in the landscape of peoplehood. Asian Americans and other racialized people become invisible and neglected. Worse, we are seen and treated as an extension of the majority culture of optimism. We become an "honorary white." An often-heard comment made about Asian Americans by white Americans is: "We have always treated you as an equal. You are no different from us." As long as Asian Americans behave according to white standards, then we can be accepted. But if we show our distinct cultural traits in relation to the white Americans, we become "inscrutable Orientals" or "the perpetual foreigners."

Difference, whether in appearance, language, behavior, value orientation, outlook on life, and wealth, becomes apparent in relationships where cruelty instead of kindness rears its head. Again, as theologian Douglas John Hall has emphasized, North Americans are an "officially optimistic society."[12] We, those who adhere to dominant norms, have a positive and progressive outlook. But those who fall outside these norms, often underprivileged or those seen as different, are inclined toward a more measured hope against hope. If the true reality of peoplehood is born through a people's relentless pursuit of life, liberty, and happiness, not only out of abundance and an optimistic hope, but equally out of their defiant hope, then countless voices crying out will be heard. John Lewis talks about "good trouble" and Japanese American artist Delphine Hirasuna talks about "*gaman*," perseverance.[13] These are the expressions that capture the meaning of defiant hope.

Pathos and anguish are many, varied, and complex, each laden with "different" people's life experiences and worldviews. Repressions of these

11. Okihiro, "Is Yellow Black or White?," 75.

12. Hall, *Lighten Our Darkness*, 43–59.

13. *Gaman* is a Japanese word for perseverance. Delphine Hirasuna in her *Art of Gaman* describes it as to "accept what is with patience and dignity" (7).

voices as "inconvenient voices" are crying out to be noticed amongst us. They arise out of the different experiences, and communities often conflicting with each other. Antipathy and liberation exist side by side. Are those whose outlook of life is optimism prepared to confront the abyss that is within us on the other side of conflicting differences? Will "We the People" be heading toward a body of neighbors, or a deeper abyss in the gathering of strangers? Furthermore, these embedded contradictions feed the entrenched oppositional, and often cruel, ways we tend to relate with each other. Can we learn to face these realities?

SPLINTERED PEOPLE: THE DEEPENING CHASM

The historical contradictions feed the way we relate with each other and are most visible in race relations. Race has always been a controversial dimension of American peoplehood. Race reveals how we have related with each other oppositionally rather than cooperatively. I contend that the current state of fragmentation and polarization we experience all around us today originates in large measure from the adversarial and hostile way of relating that is deeply built in our history from its beginning. Race relations today expose this original oppositional way of organizing our society. A case in point is the recent rise of violence against Asian Americans. To fully understand this increase in violence, we cannot ignore the incidents of "Asian African antipathy." The perpetrators of violence run across racial and ethnic lines. The visible attention paid to one group of people may unintentionally reduce the visibility of other groups. While all groups of people of color share a common pathos, at the same time there can be antipathy toward each other. This is to say that our landscape of peoplehood is far more complicated and nuanced than we traditionally assume within the black-and-white relationship dyad. Race scholars, particularly Asian American scholars, are very much attuned to this reality.

My intention in this book is not to focus alone on the Asian American experiences of race and ethnicity in our society. Rather, out of my experience I am asking, what brings people of diverse backgrounds, life formations, perspectives, values, and orientations together as people, particularly as our society is becoming much more fractured, polarized, and alienating? Since the founding days of our nation, we have been telling ourselves half-truths about our oneness in the name of "Out of Many, One." But peoplehood includes all people and their voices! We do not become "one voice."

We have not been one people, or an "us" or "we," because we have left out the participation of too many different voices in the conversation of "We the People." We have been separated and unequal one from another all these years and centuries. Now we have reached an extreme stage of separation, inequality, and alienation from one another. We inflict violence upon each other for the sake of self-interest and greed. Civil rights leader Benjamin E. Mays once said:

> I would submit that a nation cannot restore what it has not established. The nation exempted blacks and, to a large degree, native Americans from the dialectics of freedom. It has not succeeded to this day in including them. Whether blacks and other minorities will wait for the "quiet processes" to "confirm the obsolescence of our present commitments" is not just yet assured. The multiplied consequences of white racism may have created a malignancy that will not wait for such gradual and self-interested therapy.[14]

We cannot restore what we have not established. We heard the warning of separation and inequality back in the 1968 *Report of the National Advisory Commission on Civil Disorders*, otherwise called the Kerner Commission report: "Our nation is moving toward two societies, one black, one white—separate and unequal."[15] Two societies? Today what we have is multiple societies, each separate and unequal. Unless we take these warnings seriously, we will continue to perpetuate separation, inequality, and alienation. We really do not know who our neighbors are at all because we really do not share our lives together. How can we come to know our neighbors who are strangers? How can we live together? Where do we find the glue that holds us together?

At the same time, I see the yearning for and awakening of "We the People." I see it when we own up to the reality of our torn web of relationships both in our past and during the present. I believe it dwells in the hearts of people like John Lewis. In truth, it is right in the midst of the *people who realize they do not see eye to eye*. Our yearning is not merely written papers that are preserved in an archive. The awakening of a new peoplehood comes in the midst of ideas that arise out of the co-existence of antipathy and liberation. It arises out of the abyss of being treated as strangers and perhaps even as subhuman, yet holding onto the vision of seeing

14. Van Allen, ed., *American Religious Values and the Future of America*, 24–25.

15. Kerner Commission, *Report of the National Advisory Commission on Civil Disorders*, 1.

ourselves being equal, free, and just. We do not need to ask the question, what unites us into "one." Rather, we ask the question: How can "We the People" who live in a torn web relate with each other in a way that drives us toward the well-being of all, not at the expense of some? We celebrate this rebirth of peoplehood with tears of joy in the midst of deep pain. "O, yes, I say it plain, America never was America to me, and yet I swear this oath—America will be!"[16] These words of Langston Hughes speak of those who are trying to tell the "whole truth" about the story of American peoplehood in order to reach out to our neighbors.

What does it mean for us to hear the story of John Lewis? I submit that his voice presents a real portrayal of who we really are, even with our painful past and the failure to live up to what "America will be," a people created equal and free. In John Lewis, and others like him, this vision will become genuine, and compelling, inviting we the people to invest our lives in it. Hearing the unfamiliar and unpleasant voices is difficult. But by acknowledging the history and presence of these voices our hope for "We the People" will truly become convincing and authentic.

Our Declaration of Independence states, the democratic representative governance of our land derives "their just powers from the consent of the Governed." Consent is not a compromise. Consent is our common yearning for "We the People." I see this kind of bold and honest courage coming together, though long estranged, as the awakening of a renewed peoplehood, a message that echoes in my heart. The drafter of the declaration, perhaps Thomas Jefferson, commented:

> [M]ankind [*sic*] are more disposed to suffer, while evils are sufferable, than to right themselves by abolishing the forms to which they are accustomed. When a long train of abuses and usurpations, pursuing invariable the same Object evinces a design to reduce them under absolute Despotism, it is their right, it is their duty, to throw off such Government, and to provide new Guards for the future security.

Though a common interpretation of these words seems to be directed to the British empire, I hear them addressed to our own government and our own people as well. The words are self-reflective as well as accusatory of an outsider.

16. Hughes, *Collected Poems of Langston Hughes*, 191.

THE YEARNING FOR NEIGHBORS

We have been pursuing partial truths in the name of the "self-evident truths." What is illusionary is a particular historically lopsided idea of the "One" of "Out of Many." What we need to strive for is the weaving of a new web of people that has been actually hidden in our land all along. The whole truth we seek is the truth of a truly relational peoplehood, multiple, diverse, and different, but not being "one." To put it differently, we are already one people, Americans. We need to meet and respect each other. Yet this quest for a mutually respected relational people rests upon the acknowledgment of our broken peoplehood that has been with us from the founding time. I will explore our history of brokenness in the next chapter.

Today we witness polarization all around us—in our race relations, political talks, sexual identities, religious practices, and distributions of wealth. The mass shootings we witness over and over again attest to our devaluing the lives of our citizens. This devaluing of our citizens is also evident in the way we attend to the unhoused in our communities. Homelessness is not just the unavailability of affordable housing; it points to the callousness by which we treat people. We have a hard time treating all people as respected somebodies. Instead, we treat some as less than human. This is the way we separate one from another. This is the meaning of being people of contradictions. Our communities are torn apart in so many basic life locations. We seem to be paralyzed with contradictions. And yet, in the very midst of the contradictions we live, we are united as people of vision, not just an optimistic pie-in-the-sky vision of the future but the paradoxical vision of togetherness. The yearning for neighbors, rests on the realization that "no one is an island entire of itself" as poet John Donne said. At the same time, writer Frederick Buechner's words ring true:

> The paradox is that part of what binds us closer together as human beings and makes it true that no man is an island is the knowledge that in another way every man is an island. Because to know this is to know that not only deep in you is there is also such a self in me, in everyone else the world over. So, when we meet as strangers, when even friends look like strangers, it is good to remember that we need each other greatly you and I, more than most of the times we dare to admit.[17]

17. Buechner, "Pontifex," in *Hungering Dark*, 47.

We have been strangers all along, strangers who have been distanced from each other. We need to admit that we are surrounded by strangers and sojourners with their own lives full of pain and injustice. We need to further realize that another's pain is deep down just as our own pain is deep down. "We need each other greatly you and I, more than most of the time we dare to admit." This recognition can be a beginning step for the rebirth of peoplehood. This is the heart of our yearning for true peoplehood. The task ahead is to recognize the need for a collective behavioral change, a change that can lead to relating with each in a way that is an alternative to our oppositional habits. This task is multifaceted and multigenerational. The reawakening of peoplehood cannot be credibly hoped for with "optimism" alone. It requires the defiant hope, hope against hope. It requires a collective conviction of treating each one as a person, a respected human being. Such a conviction does not derive primarily from reasoned knowledge and understandings of life. It arises out of receiving the trusted stories in which we, too, are authors, just as our ancestors were lyricists.

We need a new language to speak of true peoplehood. We need a language to hear and understand the voices that speak their insights into the limitations of our shared history. We need a language that can reappreciate the vision embedded in the founding documents that speak of the "Soul of America." There are faint voices of defiant hope among the public, and familiar voices of the taken for granted aspirational hope. The voices of defiant hope speak out for equality, freedom, and justice when the lofty and buoyant ideals of optimism and progress dominate. The absent or diminished voices, as Hughes proclaims, are the voices of those

> Who made America,
> Whose sweat and blood, whose faith and pain,
> Whose hand at the foundry, whose plow in the rain,
> Must bring back our mighty dream again?[18]

These are the voices of those who relentlessly trust that reweaving the threads our republic is possible as we toil in our communal life even in the midst of our historical experiences of inequality, injustice, and alienation of one from another. As Carlos Bulosan says:

> America is not a land of one race or one class of men. We are all Americans that have toiled and suffered and know oppression and

18. Hughes, *Collected Poems of Langston Hughes*, 276.

> defeat, from the first Native American that offered peace in Manhattan to the last Filipino pea-pickers.[19]

Bulosan goes on to say that America is a "prophecy" of a renewed peoplehood. The whole truth about the story of "We the people" will emerge from hearing and bearing together the pain and defiant hope of those who are "We" but whose voices have been long neglected and ignored. American peoplehood is built on the contradictory history of "separate and equal," that is, on separate stories that are yet equally our own stories when held together. These stories both complement and contradict each other. We need a new language to hear this contradictory history of our peoplehood. This challenge, the quest for America as the prophecy of a renewed peoplehood, is so simple yet so daunting.

Something very profound is happening in our land, sometimes stealthily but also publicly at the same time. Our taken-for-granted views of peoplehood are shifting, particularly in our conversations about race as well as about gender, sexuality, class relations, and public policies. We Americans are beginning, some of us, to see ourselves through a new awakening of our hearts, not just of our heads. By now we have come to recognize the familiar words, "I cannot breathe," attributed to Eric Garner, George Floyd, and others who were caught up in police violence and died. These words go beyond the fear of having freedom and respect deprived. These words tap into primal fears of life denied, leading us to pay close attention to the previously undervalued insights into the frailty and ephemeral vision of "the City upon a Hill." These words, "I can't breathe," recognize the other side of truths that have not been "self-evident," equality, freedom, and justice of all people. "I cannot breathe" are the words for "we breathe together."

There is the story of Xiao Zhen Xie, an immigrant woman, who was suddenly attacked without provocation in broad daylight at the busy Market Street in downtown San Francisco. After the beating, her eyes were so swollen she struggled to see, and she was deeply traumatized. When her son was able to raise over a million dollars for her medical expenses through GoFundMe, Xie decided to give it all away, donating it for the cause to fight violence against Asian Americans. "We must not submit to racism, and we must fight to the death, if necessary," she said in Cantonese. The safety and well-being of her community were paramount in order for her to feel safe herself. "The issue is bigger than me," she said.[20] Yes, the issue is more than

19. Bulosan, *America Is in the Heart*, 207.

20. CBS News, "Elderly Asian Woman Who Fought Off Attack."

one single person, more than one single group or community. The issue is that of the whole peoplehood. It is the matter of "life, liberty, and the pursuit of justice." The issue is that of who we are as people and how we treat each other. These and countless other stories that have arisen out of the voiceless are signs of the awakening of our heart that we are witnessing, even if faintly, as we live in increasingly hyper-separated and unequal ways. The story of Xiao Zhen Xie joins the story of John Lewis, Eric Gardner, George Floyd, and others in the trusted story of our peoplehood. We breathe together.

CHAPTER TWO

History of Contradictions

NEVER FULLY ACHIEVED YET NEVER FORGOTTEN

So kind yet so cruel. "Is there no common denominator on which we could all meet?"[1] Bulosan meets kindhearted Americans both in his first homeland of Philippines and later in his second homeland, the US. Yet even before he reached Seattle he was called "a monkey" by white passengers on the ship. His life in America was full of violent and racist incidents as he moved from one job to another up and down the West Coast. After an incident of a beating he endured in central California, Bulosan made his way to San Jose, where he met a woman named Marian who took him in and nursed him back to health. This was the time he made the comment, "Why was America so kind and yet so cruel?" Toward the end of his life he once again traveled north from California. As the bus pulled away, he commented: "America is in [my] heart, no one can ever destroy [my] faith in America."[2]

His love of America persisted in the midst of the viciousness of life. The coexistence of contradictions lived in Bulosan's heart—and now in ours. We are a nation of contradictions. We pledge allegiance to the Republic, "one Nation under God, indivisible, with liberty and justice for all." And yet, our nation has treated powerless and unprivileged people so cruelly and continues to do so today. The history of contradictions binds us together. Kindness and cruelty, liberty and slavery, justice and the denial of

1. Bulosan, *American Is in the Heart*,19.
2. Quoted in Slater, "July Fourth."

basic human rights, breathe together in one peoplehood and in our history. We have seen ourselves as the "City on the Hill," being full of promise and believing in progress. But we have seldom appreciated the stories of Carlos Bulosan, John Lewis, and Xiao Zhen Xie. Our history tells us another story, that we are people of a torn historical fabric. The stories of those who see themselves confident of liberty, equality, and justice, even though "Never Fully Achieved," go hand in hand with the neglected stories of those who live with the memory of pain that they "Can Never Forget." Together we are people called Americans.

IN THE BEGINNING

How did the contradictions come about? How are they unfolding in our lives today? Our history gives us important clues. We see these contradictory forces engulfing this land at critical turns in our history. The history of America is the history of both kindness and cruelty that has been evolving from the two contradictory life orientations from our beginning. The evolution of the contradictions of American peoplehood began with the advent of British presence on the continent in the year 1619 with the introduction of a representative form of government—as well as slavery. The history of incongruity became codified with the birth of the nation and the establishment of a democratic form of governance in 1776. We solidified these contradictions in our societal DNA through the basic public values of privacy and freedom, which gave rise to our unique form of "individualism," which eventually gave rise to the independent "self." This history has brought about the hyper-polarization of people today who relate with each other in disparity. The current dynamics of polarization and fragmentation we experience are the culmination of these historical events and forces.

Then, in the killing of Michael Brown in Ferguson, Missouri in 2014 we found ourselves as total strangers across racial lines. We saw this one disturbing incident from totally different angles. We realized we no longer trust each other and each other's life stories. Instead, we meet each other in open conflict! Our peoplehood as we have known it is on the brink of extinction today as we react to each other out of violence. Fear, the erosion of the values that we have built and cherished for so long, and the loss of confidence in a bright future together face us as we meet the uncharted time ahead. Pursuit of happiness is relegated to the feel-good stories that appear incongruently at the end of painful stories on the nightly TV news.

THE DAWN OF CONTRASTING PEOPLEHOOD: YEAR 1619!

The arrival of Europeans in Jamestown is a controversial subject today with the publication of the *1619 Project* in *The New York Times Sunday Magazine*. The heart of the controversy is the question of what constitutes the "legitimate" history of America. The work is a collection of essays, short poems, and short stories about the legacy and implications of slavery in the USA. The project reinterprets the optimistic origin of our peoplehood. The question of America's foundation based on the stated ideals of freedom is raised when in fact America was built on the colonists' protection of their "property," the enslaved populations from the British empire. This "protection of property" created and preserved the institution of slavery and its legacy going forward. "Democracy" became the word attached to building a nation off the backs of the enslaved people in order to create the institution of slavery through the Constitution to protect the property rights of enslavers.[3] Nikole Hannah-Jones claims our founding ideals of liberty and equality were false when they were written. Black Americans fought to make them true. Without this struggle, America would have no democracy at all.[4]

> America was not yet America, but this was the moment it began. No aspect of the country that would be formed here has been untouched by the 250 years of slavery that followed. On the 400th anniversary of this fateful moment, it is finally time to tell our story truthfully.[5]

The promise of our founding ideals of liberty, equality, and justice have never been achieved without the suffering of slaves. Indeed "no aspect" of our peoplehood could have been formed here untouched by the 250 years of slavery that followed.[6] We can never forget our experiences of pain and anguish, nor should we. "Let us use history to inspire us to push a country forward, to help us believe that all things are possible and to demand a country lives up to its stated ideal," says Lonnie G. Bunch III, Secretary of the Smithsonian, commenting on the project.[7] "We the People"

3. Hannah-Jones, "1619 Project."
4. Hannah-Jones, "1619 Project," 14.
5. "1619 Project," cover page, August 18, 2019.
6. Slater, "July Fourth."
7. Bunch III, "1619 Project," back cover.

have been striving together to make the promise come true. The promise of the founders can become genuine and credible to all people when cruelty, the memory of which continues in our hearts, is owned by all.

My intent here is not only to note the major significance of the introduction of slavery to the new continent. Equally noteworthy was the introduction of a crude form of democratic governance. In other words, two major historical events took place in Jamestown in the same year. Those contradictory events set the tone of our society and have continued to imprint the character of our peoplehood ever since. Both events took place so close to each other. To be sure, historians have noted that the early representative form of government was very limited in form and substance. Only the property owners could be a representative, and the governor of Virginia could veto the bills enacted by the elected officials.

It is important to note that the introduction of slavery in 1619 was not the first such event. Earlier in 1565 the Spanish introduced enslaved Africans to present-day St. Augustine, Florida. The status of the Africans who were brought to Jamestown is also debated: Were they indentured servants who were obligated to serve for a specified period of time or indeed were they enslaved people? Notwithstanding the debate on these questions, these two historical events did indeed take place so close to each other. Our peoplehood began with a governance system conceived in liberty. Our peoplehood was also founded in the very same year as a slavocracy with the history of racial inequities that continue to this day. Our collective soul longs for a vision of a more perfect union even if it involves a slow, uncertain march toward it. At the same time our soul aches with the awareness of our long story of cruel and violent treatment of people who are at risk; a story that is embedded in the vision of liberty and equality even if we close our eyes to it. We are indeed people of contrasting stories that we live at the same time.

THE FOUNDING OF A NATION: THE NOBLE WORDS OF INVITATION THAT EXCLUDE PEOPLE

How has the story of Jamestown unfolded in the history of our peoplehood after its dawn? The founding of the nation was not a purely secular endeavor. It had a profound religious tone to it. Toward the end of the seventeenth century, the Puritans revitalized our society under the leadership of John Winthrop, Roger Conant, and others. At the same time Jonathan

Edwards, George Whitfield, and others were also seeking to renew society through the Great Awakening. The story of the religious founding this nation was later publicly declared, attributing its origin to the Divine, to the "Almighty." In the words of President Eisenhower, "In this way we are reaffirming the transcendence of religious faith in America's heritage and future; in this way we shall constantly strengthen those spiritual weapons which forever will be our country's most powerful resource, in peace or in war."[8] The "self-evident truth" of what holds people together took on a religious character. To be more precise, the religious values that underlie peoplehood in our history became more obvious.

Unlike the current diverse landscape of religious institutions and their professed values, the impact of the Protestant Puritan and Pietistic values in the seventeenth and eighteenth centuries were significant for the shaping of society and the codification of rules. Particularly noteworthy was the quest for the bright outlook of life that had a particular faith orientation embedded in the Great Awakening's notion of the New Lights and the unfolding of the divine redemption in history. The origin of the redemptive outlook of life we take for granted today, the notion that the future is brighter than the past, lies in a particular Christian theological reading of history that lies behind the foundation of our nation.

We are taught that the Declaration of Independence was a distinct way of bringing thirteen independent sovereign states into one collective peoplehood of a new republic by dissolving political differences. The well-known second sentence of the Declaration states: "We hold these truths to be self-evident, that all men are created equal, that they are endowed by their Creator with certain unalienable Rights, among these are Liberty and the pursuit of Happiness." This is a statement of values by which people of this nation strive to live together regardless of political differences. American democracy was indeed a new experiment that embodied the quest for a bright outlook of life in the future, a particular American optimism. The framework of the new nation was not dependent on the British empire as its colony. It was the establishment of a new structure, republicanism, that was totally independent of the British system with its monarchical rule. It was a republicanism "blessed" by divine providence.

The formation of American identity, expressed in the Declaration of Independence and the subsequent drafting of the Constitution and Bill of Rights, was designed to appeal to the heart of the whole republic. The

8. Eisenhower, "God in America."

language of the founding documents originated during the Protestant theological movement of the day, Puritanism, and was later reinforced through the evangelical Protestantism of the Great Awakening that dominated the mindset of the founders at the time. They were highly Christian theological documents of that day. While scholars debate the extent of the theological impact upon the founding documents, the wording of these documents mirror the religious sentiments and movements of that particular historical context for particular segments of people at the time. What brought people together, as far as the drafters of the founding documents were able to determine, was this theological framework of the day for some, but an orientation that excluded others who were then rendered invisible. Thomas Paine in his *Common Sense* saw independence rooted in Protestant beliefs that point to a distinctly American political identity.[9] Historian Sydney Ahlstrom is blunt in saying that

> By 1776 Jonathan Edwards' notion that the Kingdom of God was commencing in America had been translated by the authors of the Declaration of Independence into an official dogma: the heaven smiled upon the new nation, making it a "new order of the ages" (*e pluribus unum . . . annuit coepits . . .n ovus ordo secrum*). Jefferson, Adams, and Franklin would agree that as Israel of old had been through the wilderness to the Promised Land, so also had the United States become God's New Israel.[10] For Edwards, "the saints in heaven shall all be one society, they shall be united together without any schism, there shall be a sweet harmony, and a perfect harmony."[11]

Edwards talks about "one holy and happy society . . . relating this social vision to national covenant issues," says Gerald McDermott.[12] In other words, a personalized and egalitarian understanding of Christian faith exemplified by the "New Lights," was to be practiced rather than the institutional and formal religion of "the Old Lights." This would be the very basis of a renewed society. Life, liberty, and pursuit of happiness therefore is a theological confession of peoplehood for the founders who did not have any notion of personhood for the neglected people.

9. Rakove, *Beginnings of National Politics*, 33.

10. Van Allen, ed., *American Religious Values and the Future of America*, 7.

11. Edwards and Hickman, *Works of Jonathan Edwards*, 898.

12. McDermott, *One Holy and Happy Society*, 446

What we have come to see is that the language of equality is further articulated as the dignity of life, liberty, and the right to material stability, as a life free from the imposed life-order of the British monarchy. This language was in fact an Anglo-Saxon theological statement expressed as the political movement of the day. English Puritanism rearticulated in evangelical Protestantism formed the national consciousness of the US. The founders, Thomas Jefferson to Benjamin Franklin, were deeply steeped in an ideology of a "divinely ordained" theological heritage through which they would build a new nation, a "new Israel." This theological ideology is symbolized in the seal Thomas Jefferson proposed for the new nation. John Adams said that the seal depicts

> the Children of Israel in the Wilderness, led by a Cloud by day, and Pillar of Fire by night, and on the other Side Hengist and Horsa, the Saxon Chiefs, from whom We claim the Honor of being descended and whose Political Principles and Form of Government We have assumed.[13]

The views of God and humanity, fate and freedom, sin and hope, all provided the critical images, and at the same time alarming problems for American national life then and later. As a highly theological statement, the original notion of peoplehood as *e pluribus unum*, captured in the Declaration of Independence, emerged out of many equal sovereign states. This was a statement of a particular notion of hope, or according to the theology of Jonathan Edwards, a progressive union between the society of God's being and the society of God's saints, which is the eschatological goal of creation.[14] For the drafters of the founding documents, what brought people together was an aspirational participation in the Christian theological notion of redemption. A democratized peoplehood, full of promise, would bring different groups together in the new nation under the rule of the Divine, "one holy and happy society."[15] The foundation of oneness rests in the dignity of each individual and the equality of all people as given by the gracious Divine. This was the originating faith in the peoplehood of America that was to bring people together; a faith that increasingly ignored the differing experiences of people who are now separate and unequal in the world of increasing plurality. The founding language of equality, liberty, and justice, which was supposed to be the language of inclusion and

13. "First Great Seal Committee, July–August, 1776."

14. Michell, *Jonathan Edwards and the Experience of Beauty*, 45–46.

15. See McDermott, *One Holy and Happy Society*, 11–36.

complementarity, ignored the presence of those who were invisible and voiceless in the nascent society.

SEPARATE AND UNEQUAL

The establishment of "One people" rested in dissolving "the political bands which have connected them with another," says the Declaration of Independence. In other words, the Founders defined oneness of people as independence that is based on separation and equality, and not on codependence with the British empire. The "One people" is made up of those who come together to join God's great story of redemption in history unfolding in the new world. Just as "Israel of old had been through the wilderness to the Promised Land, so also had the United States become God's New Israel."[16] The founders of the nation set their collective hearts toward creating a society that would redeem the voiceless people who were deprived of an ability to exercise their rights under the prolonged experiences of oppression under British rule. They did so according to their faith commitments and theological understandings of human beings and society.

George Whitefield, one of the leaders of the Great Awakening, and a founder of the evangelical movement, is said to have preached to slaves and Native people as well as so-called common people of the day. Benjamin Franklin, who was said to be a religious skeptic, was captivated by Whitefield's preaching.[17] While historical circumstance excluded the participation of certain non-European populations of the day, the founding documents with their redemptive message still spoke to people's hearts, even as they do today, across the racial and other group differences.

The foundation of our society, with the hope for the equality of conditions, creates plural and diverse "opinions" that "gives birth to sentiments."[18] The now famous words of Martin Luther King Jr.—"I have a dream that one day this nation will rise up and live out the true meaning of its creed: We hold these truths to be self-evident; that all men are created equal"—attests to this appeal.[19] These words have taken a spiritual tone across our peoplehood in our multiple readings of the statement. What we need to caution ourselves about is the different meanings this public message

16. Michell, *Jonathan Edwards and the Experience of Beauty*, 45–46.

17. Bormann, *Force of Fantasy*.

18. Michell, *Jonathan Edwards and the Experience of Beauty*, 45–46.

19. King Jr., "I Have a Dream."

conveys to varied communities of people. For the privileged groups of people, the message carries an aspirational tone, one of unhampered expectation, whereas for underprivileged communities the message carries a more defiant tone—one that says "and yet" in spite of evidence to the contrary, equality and freedom persist. The same language is used, but different meanings exist across our republic. Nevertheless, it is remarkable that the public character of the language is owned by people as a whole. The contradictions of our nation are not either-or propositions; they exist together as the basic framework of our peoplehood.

All of this is to say that the foundation of our nation is not singular. It is plural and diverse from its inception. Moreover, the power of the Christian faith has not totally been eclipsed even today in our society that is increasingly multi religious and secular. The Christian narrative is an integral part of our national history and story. It tends to hold contradictory stories along with one message of redemption for all—equality, freedom, and justice, even in its parochial origin.

The very plural foundation of our peoplehood reminds us of what the majority people have never fully understood—but what the disfranchised people can never forget—which is that the majority group of our peoplehood is deeply implicated in the denial of the plurality of our nation. We are indeed separated one from another just as the spokespersons of the Great Awakening confessed—that we are all sinners. And yet, we are co-equal altogether in a complicated way, through the just God who graces each of us with dignity and life, as Jonathan Edwards and other leaders professed. Their message is that of "the separate and equal station" that holds true for all our people. Theologically it can be said of the time, "we are all sinners but are justified by grace through faith." History is spiritually redemptive in our republic. But in reality we find ourselves moving toward many societies, as the Kerner Commission states, "separate and unequal."[20]

The subtext for this accord is what is obvious: an intense aversion to bad news, and inequality's threat to freedom, and justice. To be sure, the landscape is changing. Recently we have begun to question our historical trust in the bright future. We now sense that we are somehow on the wrong track even if we cannot name what is really wrong with our peoplehood. We know we are polarized more than ever before across so many divides, race, gender and sexuality, abortion rights, gun rights, political ideologies, and beliefs. Whether this ominous trend is merely a peculiar phenomenon

20. Kerner Commission, *Report*.

of our particular age or points to a more fundamental shift in our life together as a people is yet to be known. We were divided before. However, our history tells us that we have been innately united as a forward-looking people, whether optimistic or defiant.

CONTRADICTIONS NOTICED

John Adams sounded giddy when he wrote to his wife Abigail Adams about the birth of the nation.

> The second day of July 1776 will be most memorable epoch in the history of America . . . It ought to be commemorated as the day of deliverance . . . It ought to be solemnized with pom and parade, with shows, games, sports, guns, bells, bonfires, and illuminations, from one end of this continent to the other, from this time forward forever more.[21]

Adams's wishes have been dutifully met every year ever since, not on the second day of July, but on the Fourth of July. But the public celebration is not the way Frederick Douglass viewed the Independence Day. As we have noted, he asked the now famous question:

> What to the American slave, is your 4th of July? I answer: a day that reveals to him, more than all other days in the year, the gross injustice and cruelty to which he is the constant victim. To him, your celebration is a sham; your boasted liberty, only license; your national greatness, swelling vanity; your sound of rejoicing are empty and heartless; your denunciation of tyrants, brass fronted impudence; your shouts of liberty and equality, hollow mockery; your prayers and hymns, your sermons and thanksgivings, with all your religious parade, and solemnity, are to him, mere bombast, fraud, deception, impiety, and hypocrisy—a thin veil to cover up crimes which would disgrace a nation of savages. There is not a nation on the earth guilty of practices, more shocking and bloodier, than the people of these United States, at this very hour.[22]

The two different and contradictory stories about how we understand our peoplehood have finally been named.

Rodney E. Slater calls the Declaration of Independence "contradictions of a nation," the contradictions that "pounded its chest as a champion

21. Adams, "Letter from John Adams to Abigail Adams."
22. Douglass, "What to the Slave Is the Fourth of July?"

of freedom, while enslaving an entire race and pounding their dreams into dust."[23] These contradictions describe the history of our race relations. They tell the history of our peoplehood. Publicly we say that the history of the United States is redemptive, as stated in the Constitution: "We the People of the United States, in order to form a more perfect Union, establish Justice, insure domestic Tranquility, provide for a common defense, promote the general Welfare, and secure the Blessings of Liberty to ourselves and our Posterity, do ordain and establish this Constitution for the United States of America." However, for voiceless people, particularly the minority people, our history is often tragic and painful, not redemptive, as their readings of history are often expressed in their rage. African American scholar of law Michelle Alexander puts it in the end of her book *The New Jim Crow*:

> The rage may frighten us; it may remind us of riots, uprisings, and buildings aflame. We may be tempted to control it, or douse it with buckets of doubt, dismay, and disbelief. But we should do no such thing. Instead, when a young man who was born in the ghetto and who knows little of life beyond the walls of his prison cell and the invisible cage that has become his life, turn to us in bewilderment and rage, we should do nothing more than look him in the eye and tell him the truth.[24]

Alexander echoes the word of James Baldwin in his *The Fire Next Time* when she says, truth means: "to see themselves as they are, to cease fleeing from reality and begin to change it. For this is your home, my friend, do not be driven from it."[25] One nation, one people, and yet such opposing and contradictory stories of who we are and how different are our outlooks—how we view our "home." We are indeed living in the contradictions of a nation. We are so proud of our unalienable rights of life, liberty, and the pursuit of happiness. And yet, "We the People" who "pounded its chest as a champion of freedom," we enslaved "an entire race and pound[ed] their dreams into dust."[26] One people, with many contradictory stories. Lofty words about who we are but a hollow message. The history of our people is voiced out of optimism on the one hand and voiced out of pain and anguish on the other. We are a nation "Never fully achieved" and a nation that "Can never forget."

23. Slater, "July Fourth."
24. Alexander, *New Jim Crow*, 261.
25. Baldwin, *Fire Next Time*, 5.
26. Slater, "July Fourth."

No wonder the long-held national slogan of *e pluribus unum*, "Out of Many," we become "One," sounds awfully empty and imaginary. Why are we so averse to hearing the voices that counter the public statement of the forward-looking view of peoplehood? Why do we believe only the half-truths about who we are and not the whole truth, including all our stories? Are we not aware that half-truths are the real peril to democracy because they threaten the individual rights of all? Half-truths threaten the rights of those voices that tell the life stories of tragedy as well as the rights of those who tell stories of optimism. We all suffer from this peril. As noted earlier, back in the mid-1970s Canadian theologian Douglas John Hall coined a term "officially optimistic society" to characterize American people's mind-set. This official optimism is an unofficial threat to those who tell stories of pain.

A nation of contradictions is not just a historical phenomenon limited to the founding days or the reflections of Frederick Douglass. As recently as the civil rights movement of the 1960s, we were reminded once again how divided our nation has become. Again, the 1968 Kerner Commission Report was quite prophetic about what is happening to our peoplehood today. The commission reported that both federal and state governments failed in such critical areas as providing housing, education, and social services. Then came the prophetic words that point to who we are over fifty years later: "Our nation is moving toward two societies, one black and one white—separate and unequal." These words were noted by the news media, widely reported, and noticed by the public. What was truly prophetic in the commission report came in the following words: "What white Americans have never fully understood—but what the Negro can never forget—is that white society is deeply implicated in the ghetto. White institutions created, white institutions maintain, and white society condones it."[27]

These words of the report were highly disconcerting then and are still hard to hear today, only they are even more true now. We are more divided than ever before, not only between the white communities and African American communities. Other racialized groups, Asian American and Pacific Islanders communities, Hispanic communities, Native American communities, have become more divided from each other. Not only racially but in almost every other identity group we are hyper-separated and alienated one group from another. The words—"What white society has never fully understood—but what the Negro can never forget"—can be put today as

27. Kerner Commission, *Report*, 2.

"What the majority society has never fully understood—but what all the disfranchised groups of people can never forget." We are strangers and unequal moreso than ever before. *E pluribus unum* no more! Before we even ask the question of how we can come together as a people, an urgent and dire question pressing us is this: Why have we become such strangers to each other?

WISDOM BECOMES FOLLY: THE IRONY OF AMERICAN HISTORY

To address the question of why we have become such strangers, we need to revisit the origin of the redemptive reading of history. Our history is a mixed bag of aspirations and tragedy that began in Jamestown—perhaps even before. The original intent of US independence was the redemptive righting of the wrong of British tyrannical rule. However, this intent of righting the wrong has turned out to be an expression of oppression itself, perhaps unintended. Nonetheless, the oppression of some of its own people became a fact in the new republic. This shift is well known and noted by Reinhold Niebuhr in his *The Irony of American History*. In his analysis, Niebuhr's own positivistic view of pathos, irony, and tragedy in the book cannot be ignored.

> [There are] apparently fortuitous incongruities in life which are discovered, upon closer examination, to be not merely fortuitous. . . . If virtue becomes vice through some hidden defect in virtue; if strength becomes weakness because of the vanity to which strength may prompt the mighty man or nation; if security is transmuted into insecurity because too much reliance is placed upon it; if wisdom becomes folly because it does not know its own limits—in all such cases the situation is ironic.[28]

Irony, according to Niebuhr, is the incongruity between intended codified acts and the resulting contrary consequences of the public pronouncement, an incongruity that is not coincidence but rather deeply rooted in a form of connection between act and consequences. In the history of our peoplehood what we claim to be virtue cannot be so if we consider ourselves as innocent as we pretend to be.[29] I will reflect on this irony of American history later in the segment "Redeeming the Tragic." But for now, the question of the origin of the redemptive reading of history, I

28. Niebuhr, *Irony of American History*, xxiv.

29. Niebuhr, *Irony of American History*, 19.

contend, begins with a particular Christian theological orientation that undergirded Puritanism and the Great Awakenings and was carried through by the founders of the Declaration of Independence at the beginning of the republic.

INDIVIDUALISM: THE DIGNITY OF SELF COMING HOME TO ROOST

Today we live in a highly secularized society. A Christian theological underpinning of the original civic yearning toward the "separate and equal station" of peoplehood is no longer readily agreed upon. Civil religion magnified our civic yearning for a "separate and equal" society by its religious overlay, often relying on Christian sources. But, as we continue to foster equality, freedom, and justice as the aspiration of our collective soul, knowingly or unknowingly, we also have brought about a perplexing way of relating with each other, "separate and unequal." We have done this by continuing to ignore the voices of strangers and the underprivileged. Furthermore, our civil religion has brought about the intensification of contradictions in our search for what is common. But the "separate and unequal" is not articulated in our public ideology or in the civic values of the familiar "equality, liberty, and justice." Instead, the voices of the separate and unequal arise out of the long line of people's pain and anguish that remains invisible and unheard. The search for what is common among people is no longer supported by the original theological underpinnings of our history. The search for what is common today instead takes us into unfamiliar terrain. Benjamin E. Mays, as noted earlier, says it clearly: The multiplied consequences of white racism may have created a malignancy that will not wait for such gradual and self-interested therapy.[30]

Beyond the Declaration of the Independence, the historical trend that helped solidify the contradictions of the people is individualism. Robert Bellah reminds us, "Individualism lies at the very core of American culture."[31] The contrasting and oppositional way we relate with each other is further magnified in radical individualism that is a distinct characteristic of our modern age. We assume a common virtue to be equal, free, and fair. This is what we think we all strive for. But only a certain portion of the population take part in this compact. Large groups of people are left out. Individualism

30. Van Allen, ed., *American Religious Values and the Future of America*, 24–25.

31. Bellah, "Civil Religion in America," 21.

only amplifies this discrepancy. This is so because in individualism "the self becomes the main form of reality."[32] The dignity of self is honored, somewhat eclipsing community. The value of life that upholds individualism is privacy, not living together. Because of this we start to have difficulty empathizing with what others experience.

The danger of fierce individualism was already noted by Alexis de Tocqueville. For him it is "a calm and considered feeling" of each individual citizen" content to isolate oneself from others and "withdraw into the circle of family and friends; with this little society formed to his taste, he gladly leaves the greater society to look after itself."[33] Bellah warns that radical individualism "might eventually isolate Americans one from another and therefore undermine the conditions of freedom."[34] Where did this radical individualism spring from? Bellah notes that "individualism is deeply rooted in America's social history."[35]As said before, it is embedded in the civic and religious structures of colonial life—the biblical and republican strands of John Winthrop and Thomas Jefferson as well as the utilitarian and expressive individualism represented by Benjamin Franklin as noted earlier.

We need to ask how the sacred overtone associated with freedom intersecting with individualism has played out in the oppositional way we have come to relate with each other, particularly in the dynamics of our race relations. In individualism "we the people" have lost the ability to relate with both neighbors and strangers. By lifting up individualism, the crux of the matter is not simply difference. Rather, it accentuates the state of being "separate" and unequal. Individualism, with its focus on the self, reduces our sense of civic engagement with its impulse to "get involved." The result is that strangers have become even more distanced from us, and friends less knowable.

THE SELF, NOT RELATIONSHIP BECOMES THE MEASURE OF REALITY

With the founding of the new nation, "independence" meant self-determination, freedom, and not having to live under the thumb of somebody else. This is what the image of the new nation was all about. This image is really a

32. Bellah et al., *Habits of the Heart*, 143.
33. Tocqueville, *Democracy in America*, 508.
34. Bellah et al., *Habits of the Heart*, viii.
35. Bellah et al., *Habits of the Heart*, 147.

revolt against the dominion of another power, or the insistence of our own will to power, whether it be a political or some divine rule to chart the life of people. This is the image of a society that creates its own laws and regulations that guide the conduct of its government without intervention from a foreign state. Yet, the equality of social conditions "creates opinions" and "gives birth to sentiments," says Tocqueville. As such, equality is really the "primary fact" about America from which our style of democracy derives and functions.[36] Perhaps we can begin to see the contradiction and eventual conflict that will arise as these forces begin to clash with each other.

I would argue that there is a critical difference between what the founders of the nation understood about the nature of independence and the way Tocqueville described the meaning of democracy. For the founders, history was redemptive in the way Reinhold Niebuhr talks about faith and history. The republic is redemptive not because its people strive toward redemption (an expression of individualism) but rather the republic is redemptive because people join the history that moves toward God's redemption (an expression of cooperative equality). A republic that is interpreted as redemptive reflects the redemptive story described in the Christian faith in which we, too, join in its unfolding. Redemption, in other words, is to be believed, assumed, trusted, and most importantly joined for its realization by the populace, not something to be created and achieved by their own efforts.

Tocqueville, on the other hand, describes the "equality of conditions" that "creates opinions" as the generative rule of life for American democracy. In other words, Tocqueville understood democracy and the dignity of the self as the foundation of American peoplehood. For Tocqueville, America is redemptive because its people by their own effort "create" plural and diverse "opinions." In this view America is not initiated and guided by divine providential power. The theological affirmation of the divine movement in the founding of this nation on the one hand, and civil governance molded out of plural voices in the society of individuals in the culture of individualism on the other hand, reveal a fundamental contradiction that plays neatly into the rise of individualism, where "the self becomes the main form of reality."

The meaning and basic assumptions of redemptive history shift in Tocqueville's reading, supporting the emerging and stronger American identification with individualism. The self as the focus of reality fosters a kind of contentment to isolate our independent selves from each other and "withdraw into our circle of family and friends. With this private little society

36. Tocqueville, *Democracy in America*, 508.

formed to our taste, we gladly leave the greater society to look after itself."[37] Bellah warns that radical individualism "might eventually isolate Americans one from another and therefore undermine the conditions of freedom."[38] As we move further and further away from our neighbors, we become more and more strangers. The act of trusting people becomes increasingly difficult, as well as our trust of ourselves. This culture of individualism has only intensified the contradictions we inherited and live with today.

It is interesting to note how individualism and freedom have been linked to the history of what it means to be an American. Robert Bellah recounts the insights of St. John de Crevecoeur, a French settler and author of *Letter from an American Farmer*. In this letter, Bellah notes the revealing insight into the unique role entrepreneurship plays as it is associated with individual initiative, thus cementing its relationship to personal freedom in becoming an American. In the name of individual initiative and freedom, the transformation occurs as the European immigrant becomes an American:

> From nothing to start into being; from a servant to the rank of a master; from being the slave to some despotic prince, to become a free man, invested with lands, to which every municipal blessing is annexed! What a change indeed! It is in consequence of that change that he becomes an American.[39]

Freedom is indeed a "most resonant, enduring American value."[40] People as a whole have enjoyed freedom as an American value. But it is true that there are segments of American society where freedom is not at hand. This means that the equilibrium between trust in the future which has "never been fully achieved" and the memories of cruelty that some people "can never forget," has become precarious indeed. In the world of the exaggerated individual self, embedded in unequal power dynamics, the impact of this inflated self on others makes community relations precarious, especially when it comes to race relations. Those who take the primacy of the individual self for granted are particularly vulnerable to its negative impact on others. Reinhold Niebuhr reminded us, "if wisdom becomes folly because it does not know its own limits," then we find ourselves today in the ironic situation for democracy. The communication and relationships

37. Tocqueville, *Democracy in America*, 508.

38. Bellah et al., *Habits of the Heart*, viii.

39. J. Hector, St. John de Crevecoeur, *Letters from an American Farmer*, 83.

40. Bellah et al., *Habits of the Heart*, 23.

across the lines of contradictions become increasingly laborious when "self" becomes the foundation of measuring reality.

THE FERGUSON EFFECT: CONTRADICTIONS ERUPT INTO OPEN AND VIOLENT CONFLICT

When individualism invades the soul of America it wreaks havoc in relationships already steeped in fundamental contradictions. With the individual self now the dominant measure of reality in a culture already polarized by contradictions, further complications arise when this self is embodied in a white body. That self, then, not only defines reality but defines it through white reality. This in turn reinforces white privilege and white supremacy, which means that other voices become not only marginalized, but inconsequential. How then do we communicate and relate with each other across the lines of difference, particularly racial differences?

Today, difference is no longer the presence and inclusion of different points of view. Individualism and its manifestation in the individual self, embodied in the white body, has accentuated the centrality of power relations involved in our ongoing "contradictions." Our history tells us that different and conflicting readings of events have become devalued and denied in public decision-making as differences are increasingly reflecting racial differences. Difference has become a matter of whose voice counts and who controls the power to decide the future. Decision-making is being carried out by denying the "inconvenient" voices and views in order to secure the sovereignty of the dominant group. The counter-voices are silenced and rendered "inconsequential" because they threaten the authority of dominant, white, individual selves. As a result, the individual dominant hyper-self reinforces the adversarial and sometimes violent way we relate with each other. Consider a case in point, that of Michael Brown Jr.

On August 9, 2014, Michael Brown Jr., an unarmed African American youth, was killed in Ferguson, Missouri, a suburb of St. Louis, by a white police officer, Darren Wilson. The question became whether or not the killing was justified. Wilson, who was white, perceived Brown as uncooperative and a dangerous threat. He was convinced that the circumstances justified killing Michael. The black witnesses saw Michael as a scared and vulnerable suspect, not threatening or dangerous to the arresting officer. *The New York Times* reported a year later:

> The shooting prompted protests that roiled the area for weeks. On Nov. 24, the St. Louis County prosecutor announced that a grand jury decided not to indict Mr. Wilson. The announcement set off another wave of protests. In March, the Justice Department called on Ferguson to overhaul its criminal justice system, declaring that the city had engaged in constitutional violations.[41]

What evidence was presented about the altercation at the police car? And what witnesses described Michael Brown's movements? These are the questions presented by *The New York Times* reporters. To this question, the article says: "The St. Louis County prosecutor said the most credible witnesses reported that Mr. Brown charged toward the officer."[42] The decision of the grand jury not to indict Wilson brought about a series of protests. *The Times* summarized the incident: "The protests against the police have pitted the predominantly black community against a nearly all-white police force. Of the 53 commissioned officers in the Ferguson Police Department, four are black."[43] Black people did not think Michael instigated the conflict. White police believed he did. A white judge and predominantly white jury agreed and sided with the officer, silencing the black voices, rendering them "inconsequential."

This incident was interpreted in radically different ways and produced an outcome based on differing perspectives and readings of reality. What was once termed the Rashomon Effect can now be replaced by what I would term the "Ferguson Effect." The original Rashomon Effect says that an event is given contradictory interpretations or descriptions by those who witness it, giving different perspectives of the same incident. The Rashomon Effect alone would suggest different readings based on contradictory historical realities, much as the dominant celebration of the Fourth of July was refuted by the somber interpretation by Frederick Douglass. The Ferguson Effect brings the power differentials into the interpretations, a power differential heightened by an inflated "self" operating from the advantaged and privileged side of individualism.

The different interpretations of the Michael Brown killing became acutely polarizing as they pit the Ferguson police department against the black community. It became further divisive as the reality of whose voices mattered, whose voices had authority, whose voices were heard became

41. *New York Times*, "What Happened in Ferguson."

42. *New York Times*, "What Happened in Ferguson."

43. *New York Times*, "What Happened in Ferguson."

evident. In the end, the power of the individual voice of an individual white officer supported by individual white onlookers carried the day. Different historical experiences informed conflicting interpretations of this case while the power of an inflated white "self" sealed it. In the wake of the killing of a black citizen, the Black Lives Matter movement emerged and became a new cry for justice.

Some have seen the Black Lives Matter movement as a threat, not merely a threat to white extremists by the so called "deep left conspiracy," but also as a threat to the taken-for-granted notion that America is "the Land of the Free and the Home of the Brave." A notion deeply embedded in the soul of America while at the same time a soul distorted by white privileged individualism.

The fear of whites toward people of color arises in part out of their privileged interpretations of the soul of America based on their also privileged perspectives of life, liberty, and the pursuit of happiness. The fears of whites then become complicated by a soul being shaped by the shift toward radical individualism with its taken-for-granted privileged voice and power. Many whites fear their ways of life, now encapsulated in a more individualistic and private way of living, will become threatened, invalidated with the possibility of their power base becoming destabilized—if previously silenced voices become heard. This clash of experiences, worldviews, and social formations make compromise or consensus extremely difficult, if not impossible.

As noted throughout this book, people of color do not generally share the same notion of the soul of America as the taken-for-granted views of the dominant culture—a soul free of contradictions and unencumbered by the inflated and isolated self. People of color more often have a suspicion of this "soul," having been on the receiving end of its abuse of power,

At the societal level, individualism, embodied in a white self, functions as the absence of conversation across the lines of power differences, an absence driven by fear. It makes any practice of "consent" extremely difficult because the power imbalance of separate and unequal prevails. This is what the "Ferguson Effect" points to: We fear each other and choose not to engage in conversation because we really don't know each other. We do not wish to hear other people's life stories, their struggles, and insights that are born of their pain of struggles. Therefore, we choose not to be in relationship with each other. As Martin Luther King Jr. once said, "I am convinced that men hate each other because they fear each other. They fear each other because they don't communicate with each other, and they don't communicate with each other because they are separated from each other."[44] The separation becomes legitimized in official judicial decisions, which further aggravate the division and distrust between opposing communities. This is a sad outcome of the fundamental and historical contradictions that we live with as they are filtered through the eyes of our isolated and distorted individual selves.

The disturbing outcome of the Ferguson Effect, as we begin to see its multilayered reality, is that we are becoming increasingly suspicious and hostile in relating with each other on an interpersonal level as well as in our hyperpolarized group and public life. Perhaps the Ferguson Effect can give us some fresh understanding as to why we are moving toward such a profoundly fragmented society, a "separate and unequal" people. All around us we witness fragmentation in the hostility and violence against people of color and other minoritized people. And we ask why must we continue to push others away with an intent to hurt, or worse, to eliminate them? Furthermore, why do we continue to legitimize the decisions rendered by government agencies that perpetuate violence and hold divisions in place?

For example, the conversation involving Black Lives Matter is no longer the reminder of dignity, equality, well-being, and justice for African Americans. Instead of seeing its multilayered history and contexts, it is now treated as different readings of law enforcement and policing policies—as in the Michael Brown case. Justice gets camouflaged and debased in the guise of differences of opinions on race and racism. Race is even being cast as a "patriotic" ideological movement by white supremacists who use their definitions of race against the opposing political movement, with false conspiracy myths of assaults against law enforcement officials and agencies by people of color. In this confrontative politics, power dynamics become inverted.[45] The treatment of race and racism in such a toxic context becomes even more highly politicized, shifting the focus to power policy differences and away from the historical notion of racial and social justice. These factors might continue to plague us until we finally become so deeply distrustful and hateful of each other that we assume we no longer need each other.

Reinhold Niebuhr exposed the magnitude of our "inclination to injustice" in our common positivistic heart. The now familiar words of Niebuhr still speak to us: "Man's capacity for justice makes democracy possible, but

44. King Jr., "Speech Given in King Chapel."

45. See Goodreads, "White Feminism Quotes."

man's inclination for injustice makes democracy necessary."[46] Inequality and injustice need to be tamed within the structure of democracy. Democracy is a powerful expression of peoplehood that subdues our "inclination for injustice," that is, our thirst for the welfare of individual selves. This is the basic underlying assumption behind justice in the US.

Niebuhr's understanding of the role of democracy arises out of his Christian theological view of the centrality of the cross, which exposes the inherent "self-interested power" of human beings, says theologian James Cone.[47] In a societal setting, people are "immoral." That is, they have a limited capacity to go beyond self-interest to see the society from the point of view of the well-being of others. This self-centered inclination is expressed as the will to power. Human power does not concede without struggle, as Niebuhr famously articulated. It is power of one over another in unbalanced power dynamics. Democracy, then, is the means to chasten this raw power. It regulates the human impulse for power over, violence, and hopefully puts power towards mutual ends. This is Niebuhr's view of "Christian realism." It originates, in his view of the centrality of the divine power of love, the theological standpoint that is deeply steeped in the prevailing neo-orthodox theology of his days. For Niebuhr, the divine love is the absolute yardstick by which all human motives and actions are measured and judged. Human beings are not capable of replicating divine love due to our inclination toward self-interest. Divine love is what Niebuhr calls the "impossible possibility."[48]

While the divine love expressed in the event of the cross is central to Niebuhr's understanding of Christian faith, it does not readily work in the political power struggles and the policies that regulate them in a secular age. For Niebuhr, we can only approximate love in the form of justice. Justice, then, approximates divine love under the conditions of human inclinations toward self-interest expressed in power.

In addition, Niebuhr's observation does not adequately address the heart of race relations and racism in the US today, with its built-in contradictions of the experiences of people of color resulting in separate and unequal relationships. What appears to be assumed in Niebuhr's realism of approximate justice of American democracy raises a critical question: Does justice, even if it is approximately expressed, need to be enacted as power

46. Niebuhr, *Children of Light and Children of Darkness*, 118.

47. Cone, *Cross and the Lynching Tree*, 35.

48. Niebuhr, *Interpretation of Christian Ethics*, 109.

of one over another? To put it differently, does justice need to be confined within the structures of the existing coercive and adversarial dynamic of power relationships, and struggles that undermine a balanced web of humanity? Granted the struggles for equality and justice have been fought in the realm of power struggles. But this approach could end up replicating the structure of oppositional power dynamics, not questioning the structure of relations itself.

> We take, and must continue to take, morally hazardous actions to preserve our civilization. We must exercise our power. But we ought neither to believe that a nation is capable of perfect disinterestedness in its exercise, nor become complacent about particular degrees of interest and passion which corrupt the justice by which the exercise of power is legitimated.[49]

". . . the exercise of power is legitimated," says Niebuhr. A case in point is the recent assault on the US Capitol by those who were willing to bypass the democratic process of the governance of the people. Does "approximate justice" based on consent really function today to safeguard democracy against violent acts? To put this question differently, does the current polarization in our existing oppositional way of life condone questionable "morally hazardous actions" that inflict violence and bypass the democratic system? I have a hunch that it does.

In the absence of an analysis and critique of the existing pattern of oppositional relations, we are at risk not only of perpetuating polarizations among diverse groups, but of exacerbating the power imbalance, which perpetuates hostility between them as well. In the increasingly separate and unequal worlds of people, violence becomes the tempting means to settle the imbalance of power. When one group is given the power of privilege that is not afforded another or marginalized groups, James Cone reminds us that "Niebuhr's moderate view was not one to empower a powerless group to risk lives for freedom."[50] When the majority-race political leaders falsely portray the cities with a sizeable population of people of color as places suspected of voting fraud, they are pandering to white supremacists who do not see the power imbalance between themselves and people of color. This is power privilege! Power privilege within the framework of an adversarial epistemology functions both overtly and in an indirect fashion. It can lead to blatant violence as we have witnessed in so many arenas of

49. Niebuhr, *Irony of American History*, 118.

50. Cone, *Cross and the Lynching Tree*, 71.

life, from the incidents of racially tinged police violence to alleged voting fraud, and personal violence against racial minority people. And it can lead to insidious violence where children are obliquely deprived of adequate education and their parents' healthcare. The power imbalance built into the systems of relations is undermining the democratic system!

REDEEMING THE TRAGIC: A FRESH WAY OF FRAMING THE FUTURE OF PEOPLEHOOD

If violence, fragmentation, and mistrust mark our current national landscape, the question continues to be, where do we go from here as a people? What might redeeming our faith in our future together look like? I still contend that the beginning chapter of the story of a new peoplehood is our own history of contradictions: Why is America both kind and cruel? Why is the Fourth of July at once the day of deliverance for some and the day to mourn for others? A large portion of "We the People" continue to hold on to a faith in redemptive history, while the overlooked segments of our population have been living tragic lives and find the motto "One out of Many" arbitrary, illusionary, and anachronistic. These divisive forces expose the frivolity of any officially optimistic faith.

Our history reminds us that our nation has been moving toward separate societies, one society with an unquestioned faith in a positivistic reading of history, while another experiences the pathos and tragedy of separate and unequal. In other words, we speak different languages about our peoplehood. As a result, our nation is indeed moving toward a more fragmented and polarized society. To paraphrase the Kerner Commission's report, the awful truth is: What majority Americans have never fully understood—but what unprivileged people can never forget—is that the majority-controlled society is deeply implicated in creating the ghetto. Their institutions created it. Their institutions maintained it. And their society condones it.[51] This lies at the heart of our fragmented peoplehood created by our history of contradictions. The reality of American peoplehood today is the coexistence of those who don't understand the reality of contradictions and those who have a deep memory of the contradictions in their hearts. Will we acknowledge the presence of this contradiction? Will we be able to live with this foundation of our peoplehood in order to chart our way into the future?

51. *Report of the National Advisory Commission*, 2.

The question of where we go from here begins, then, with the acknowledgment of the contradictions we have fashioned in our nation's history. This is a daunting challenge, indeed perhaps impossible. There is no quick and simple response to this question of the future of our peoplehood. Furthermore, to make the separate and unequal state of peoplehood a shared reality of all people, we need to accept the oppositional and adversarial ways we have been relating with each other all along. Individualism is not simply the absence of relationality, it is a particular and peculiar way of relating with our neighbors. The sacrality of liberty or freedom that is interpreted as our inherent right to manage our own lives is based on our peculiar way of treating our neighbors as an outsider, a stranger, or even as an enemy. We don't seem to be able to recognize our neighbor as someone who is really a part of who we are, another human being with whom we share a living relational web.

Our assumed notion of the sacrality of freedom, as well as our individualism, makes the acknowledgment of the contradictions of our history harder. The notion of individualism is a tacit view that assumes that we possess and therefore can manage our own beings with our own ability and freedom, rather than a view that we receive our being by living with others in a relational web.[52] In other words, the idea of individual ownership of our own beings and self-interests lie behind our belief in the sacrality of freedom. The self is not only the measure of reality, the self is also exceptionally sacred and dignified. This view leads to the belief that what is owned needs to be defended with the help of those who are like-minded from those who would threaten to take it away from us. This antagonistic way of relating with others, evident in today's fragmentation and polarization, is deeply embedded as an unexamined framework of our society that organizes the way we live and relate with each other. It can be said that the dualistic and oppositional epistemology that structures our relationships brings no harmony and complementarity, and in fact is becoming a major threat to all our well-being.

The danger of radical individualism that Tocqueville, Bellah, and others warned us about cannot adequately be understood without recognizing the presence of this epistemological underpinning of the ownership of self. The danger of radical individualism needs to be seen as the undercurrent feeding our common life in order to fully evaluate its impact. The danger of a reified individualism and the quest for purely private fulfillment not

52. Hall, *Lighten Our Darkness*, 81.

only serves to isolate us from one another and undermine the conditions of freedom; more alarmingly, it might result in violence against the "other" that could ultimately threaten the very existence of our peoplehood. Our unexamined faith in redemptive history along with its aspirational trust in the future could result in a permanent and dangerous "separate and unequal" state of people. Freedom that was originally meant to promote respect for an individual's rights without the tyranny of the majority has now become a freedom that provides no limit to what one can say or do. This reified understanding of "freedom at all costs" means the protection of our individual selves from an encroachment by others. This has become our "fundamental right." It is good to remember that the preamble to the US Constitution says that the establishment of the federal government is to "secure the Blessings of Liberty to ourselves and our Posterity." Freedom as it was originally understood meant that individuals could enjoy it within the context of a civil society with a constitutionally representative government. It is therefore named "civil liberty." Today freedom is tearing the web of people apart that is supposed to bring us together in a "civil" fashion. Unmoored "Freedom" has come home to roost!

So once again, we need to ask ourselves: Where do we go from here? It cannot be disputed that the contradictions of expectations and experience are endangering our web of relationships. A viable future will depend on whether or not we can mend the tattered web of peoplehood that is built on contradictions and the notion of individual freedom within a framework of unequal power dynamics. Countless stories from historical faith traditions throughout the world give us valuable insights about where a new well-being of people can begin. The insights are often born out of the heart of the night and not under the bright daytime sun. Life under the sun is often the story of half-truths. Life that we are awakened to in the middle of night gives us something we cannot readily see under the daylight sun. The stories of anguish and pain are nighttime stories, difficult to hear, sometimes taken as voices of self-pity. But even as they are haltingly told these stories of aches and rage, of being a neglected "We," bring very faint lights that illuminate what we are unable to see under the bright daylight. The future of our peoplehood could benefit from this wisdom, a wisdom from the night, the night of the broken heart.

Pastoral theologian Sharon Thornton sees America as "America of the Broken Heart."

> When I listen to the words of our two "national anthems," it seems to me as though many Americans live out the vision of "The Star-Spangled Banner." It is a vision of triumph, of pride in success, that communicates a certain confidence and assurance. This is the hymn of a proud heart. It is a heart unable to be touched by the pain of God. The vision of the second heart doesn't seem so clear. "My country, 'tis of thee, sweet land of liberty," suggests a place where the climate of true civility thrives. The hymn of letting freedom ring sings of a vision still to be realized. Therefore, it is a hymn of the broken heart.[53]

Her insights into the realizing the America of the heart were born out of her listening the people of the broken heart.

Theologian H. Richard Niebuhr also approached history as the history of the heart. This understanding of history is critical in recognizing the "neglected side of the contradictions," an unappreciated side of the story of American people. In this age of contextualized approaches to faith understandings, Niebuhr's *The Meaning of Revelation* may well be viewed as a product of bygone era with the musty smell of an old book. But I find the message of the book quite insightful in framing the discussion of the future of American peoplehood. Particularly as it gives us a helpful insight into the need to listen to the voices of the brokenhearted.

To be sure, for Niebuhr "Revelation" means the Christ event, the story of Jesus as told in numerous ways throughout the history of Christianity. To be sure, he is not referring to the voices of the voiceless when he explains the meaning of revelation. However, in his explanation of the story of Jesus, he helps us understand what it means to approach the history of American peoplehood, particularly to hear the voices of those who are not speaking of the "officially optimistic" posture of life. When Niebuhr talks about "history as lived and as seen," he is speaking about the history that speaks to our heart, really our broken heart, not a history that is written and appeals only to our head. The meaning of the revelation, the story of the Christ event is that

> something has happened to us in our history which conditions all our thinking and that through this thinking we are enabled to apprehend what we are, what we are suffering and doing and what our potentialities are. What is otherwise arbitrary and dumb fact

53. Thornton, *Broken Yet Beloved*, 213.

> becomes related, intelligible and eloquent fact through the revelatory event.[54]

It is almost like by listening to a "hymn of the broken heart," we bear witness to a "history as lived," a history that speaks to our hearts even if we try to hide that particular history. The "hymn" guides us to reimagine the familiar words of the founders of the republic in light of the experiences of the brokenhearted. They "hum" the experiences that are hard to hide even if we try, the unspeakable pain and anguish of living in the land of official optimism. These are the voices that hum, moan, speak the inconvenient truths of life and history. Listening to them could "condition all our thinking" and enable us to apprehend who we are, what we are suffering and doing, and what our potentialities might be. In other words, the voices of the brokenhearted illuminate the depth and weight of our public declaration of who we are as people who seek life, liberty, and the pursuit of happiness. These venerated, familiar words might become genuine, compelling, and rearticulated, inviting people to invest their lives in them. In this sense, the historically neglected voices are truly "revelatory." In the words of Sharon Thornton,

> For those who have not experienced historical injuries, it will mean receiving the tears of others who have—until those tears wear away all false pretentions of ever being free from the legacy of historical atrocities. It will mean realizing that there is no such thing as historical innocence. This means that no one of us can ever "go home" again, and our new "home" is still a future-leading image.[55]

Delving into the world of the voiceless is a courageous act, not easily done if in fact done at all. Hear the words of James Baldwin addressed to his nephew in his *The Fire Next Time:*

> [T]his is your home, my friend, do not be driven from it, great men have done great things here, and will again, again can make America what it must become. It will be hard, but you come from sturdy peasant stock, men who picked cotton and dammed rivers and built railroads, and, in the teeth of the most terrifying odds, achieved an unassailable and monumental dignity. You come from a long line of great poets since Homer. One of them said, The very time I thought I was lost, My dungeon shook and my chains

54. Niebuhr, *Meaning of Revelation*, 1941.

55. Thornton, *Broken Yet Beloved*, 212.

> fell off. We cannot be free until they are free. God bless you, and Godspeed.[56]

Listen to James Baldwin's voice. He speaks the other side of half-truths. If we really listen, we might hear that it is the voice of an unfamiliar neighbor of ours providing "us with an image by means of which all the occasions of personal and common life become intelligible" in a way they were not before.[57] His voice and the voices of countless other formerly voiceless people shine by their own lights. To closely paraphrase Niebuhr's words, they are intelligible in themselves while they illuminate other events and enable us to understand them.[58] Of course, it would be naïve to assume that the revelatory voices can be readily heard in the way Niebuhr describes. There are some, perhaps, many, who would say that these stories of the brokenhearted are not their stories at all. To some they may not be stories that illuminate "what is otherwise arbitrary and dumb fact." All the same, we need to pay attention to a new art of listening.

56. Baldwin, *Fire Next Time*, 10.

57. Niebuhr, *Meaning of Revelation*, 80.

58. Niebuhr, *Meaning of Revelation*, 80.

PART TWO

The Counter-Habits of the Heart

LISTENING TO THE VOICES OF THE BROKENHEARTED

THE MESSAGE OF THIS book is that we are divided in the intrinsic ways we view and live out who we are as a people. In the history of our peoplehood, we have related with our neighbors in oppositional ways. Today these ways of relating are becoming so raw that sometimes we are unable to relate with each other at all across the lines of difference. We forget that we are people living together even in the contrary ways that we meet each other. We call this polarization. The warning of Alexis de Tocqueville in the middle of the nineteenth century has become our contemporary reality. He warned that a society of highly differentiated individuals would eventually lack social structures to help mediate relations with the state. This could easily result in a democracy in which the well-being of "We the People" becomes undermined by powerful groups of people who have accrued inordinate power. Given this scenario, I ask these questions: Why do we need to listen to the stories of strangers whose lives are painful, tragic, and powerless? Why do we need to communicate with our neighbors who are strangers? Why do we need to do so when we are convinced that the future is bright? The answer to these questions lies in the act of listening, particularly listening to unfamiliar and uncomfortable stories. This simple yet profound practice of really listening just may lead us to realize that we are a people of the broken heart and a fragmented soul.

We understand ourselves as an optimistic people who believe that our problems will be solved if we continue to keep trying. Yet, living with contradiction is the more accurate description of the state where we find ourselves today. Contradictions break people apart. A people of the broken heart, then, is a fitting depth meaning of how we live together. The broken heart points to the counter-habits of heart that quietly have existed in our history along with the more taken-for-granted and unexamined habits of the heart. To know that we are broken in the way we meet our neighbors is to know that we can also be kind rather than cruel, less confrontational and adversarial. To know that we are people of a broken heart is to know the possibility of an alternative way of being with each other. Martin Buber suggests this when he talks about an "I" who relates with another as a subjective "Thou" instead of an objective "it." He talks about people as being relational, "I-Thou." We are each the "I" who is related to the Thou of another person, not the over against an objectified "It."[1]

To know that we are people of a broken heart is an act of taming the tyranny of the powerful, for the health and well-being of all people. This is particularly true in a society where the "intermediate social structures that mediate relations with the state" are increasingly becoming fragile, perhaps even more so than in the time of Tocqueville. Today community polarization is an alarm bell, warning of the ultimate demise of our legitimate rights as the value of personal liberty becomes threatened for everyone. Hyper-separation combined with the unequal treatment of people is tearing the whole society apart in the name of a distorted historical reading of freedom, a distortion that is now turning freedom into a vice. The brokenness of our communal heart is a "revelation" that has emerged in our midst. And yet, who admits the state of our peoplehood?

The central challenge facing us today is to admit in our deep collective heart that there is a large gap between the vision of who we believe ourselves to be as a united people and who we actually are. This gap reveals the reality that we are estranged in a state of unacknowledged and unequal differences. We are already a gathered people who live together, *e pluribus unum*, but this means we are a people of contradictions, both kind and cruel. We need to grieve these contradictions and all the pain they have engendered in order to reweave this web of our "broken yet beloved" people for our future.[2]

We long for a healthy relational peoplehood where we care for each other. By owning up to the brokenness of our relationships that have been

1. Buber, *I and Thou.*

2. See Thornton, *Broken Yet Beloved.*

with us from our beginning, we might find a new way forward. This is not an optimistic unfolding of history, rather a radical hoping for a future that is not self-evident. Our healing, in the words of Martin Luther King Jr., will involve trusting that "one day on the red hills of Georgia, the sons of former slaves and the sons of former slave owners will be able to sit down *together* at the table of brotherhood."[3] Our faith in justice and the yearning for equal and free opportunities becomes more authentically revealed when we admit the nightmare of our history of denied equality, freedom, and justice. "Why is America so kind and so cruel?" Can we own this "tragic gap"?[4] This is a daunting challenge indeed. Daunting because the reawakening of peoplehood begins with the admission of the actual unbalanced, estranged, and broken state of our collective life. As long as there are a sizeable number of people for whom race and racism, as well as other unequal differences, are treated as a "matter of choice" that does not need acknowledgment, the future of our peoplehood will continue to exist in its current broken state, a state where the separation of people and their unequal treatment will become even more pronounced.

When the actual experiences of people and communities are profoundly asymmetrical and disconnected, how do we dissolve the political and societal barriers in order to say "yes" to a people living together amidst differences? How do we say "yes" to the *unum*, that is inherently unstable and yet intended to meet the needs of all people equality at any given time? *E pluribus unum* rests on this premise, "Out of many, one." This is an operational language that calls for negotiation among differences in order to be true to the society that is currently "separate and unequal." Yet, even in a separate and unequal history the term "separate and equal" cannot be etched into stone as some eternal truth about who we are. The truth *unum* of *E pluribus unum* rests on the multitude of stories we tell about who we are. *Unum* involves a multiple truth! Our true peoplehood involves our multiplicity with all our divergent experiences, views, values, and hopes. And this will involve our ongoing negotiations and adjustments with one another over and over again in time.

Differences with the imbalance of power are built into the foundation of our peoplehood. "One" seems to state the obvious. We are one gathered group of people, bringing together all our different viewpoints, life experiences, stories, and power statuses that make up our journey. "One" is also

3. King Jr., "I Have a Dream."

4. From Palmer, *Healing the Heart of Democracy*.

the reality of our collective history of contradictions. It is not the future we strive for. It is who we are as a people. Therefore, the Declaration of Independence reminds us of the need for "a decent respect for the opinions of (all) mankind." In the meantime, we remain different and separate and unequal while at the same time we are together on a journey. Our life together rests on the negotiated "consent" of the governed. As the Constitution states, "One" is really the given reality of who we are, separate and unequal. This includes all people who are on journey together toward what we say that we are—the land of equality, freedom, and justice. We profess this in the midst of our contrary experiences of both kind and cruel, separate and unequal. What holds us together? The answer is that we are journeying together, even though we are unjust and unequal in our treatment of one another. This is our lived reality of "One out of many."

Earlier in Part One I suggested that an alternative to an oppositional way of relating with each other is a complementary way. I do not mean to suggest that a complementary way of relating can completely replace the oppositional way we Americans have related with each other. That is not my intention. We are people of contradictions, a people who have valued individual freedom even while we have not treated our neighbors well. We cannot go back and reverse the way we have related in our history. But we can ask what this means for our life together in the future. The language of equality, freedom, and justice—life, liberty, and the pursuit of happiness—is what we call the language of our dominant habits of the heart. These habits are not some abstract ends and goals for which we strive. They are what our journey together is all about, a journey imbued with contradictions that eclipse the neglected counter-habits of the heart. These contradictions are the glue that held people together in the past as they continue to hold us together today. They reveal the way our American journey has unfolded. How can they be tamed for a future where all can become recipients of a more authentic life, liberty, and the pursuit of happiness?

The account of our peoplehood, whose underpinnings were initially informed by a particular theological confession of "Christian America," took place amidst the cruel treatments of people as slaves and other displaced strangers. This meant that not all people were included in this initial forming of our country's citizenship. These first habits of the heart later morphed into the image of an all-encompassing "soul" of America often understood as civil religion.

Robert Bellah, a critic of our taken-for-granted habits of the heart, talks about the religious origins influencing our idea of authority. He calls this process of incorporating religious assumptions into our civic life "reification." Bellah identified the American Revolution, the Civil War, and the civil rights movement as three decisive historical events that impacted the content and imagery of what has become civil religion in the United States. These historical events reveal how through reification,

> "The American civil religion was never anticlerical or militantly secular. On the contrary, it borrowed selectively from the religious tradition in such a way that the average American saw no conflict between the two. In this way, the civil religion was able to build up without any bitter struggle with the church powerful symbols of national solidarity and to mobilize deep levels of personal motivation for the attainment of national goals."[5]

Perhaps without any maleficent intent, the dominant habits of the heart have turned into violent actions, as seen in the assassinations of our leaders and even ordinary people in recent decades. We might even say the dominant habits became pointedly distorted and harmful in the attack on our nation's capital after the 2020 presidential election. The adversarial dynamic of the way we relate has become intensified and hyper-individualized in acts of violence. What impact does the reification of a civil religion, as expressed in the addition by President Dwight D. Eisenhower in 1954, to our Pledge of Allegiance "one nation under God," have on our public life? Our public life has reached the level of violence today that is shattering our societal coherence. This makes the questions about the absent voices in our history we have been considering even more significant. What role can the stories of our broken heart, with their counter-habits of the heart, play for our peoplehood today and in the future? Can we recover and redeem these stories of our heart for all our sake? More importantly, can we appreciate the potential healing for our collective troubled spirits arising out of both the familiar habits of the heart and the counter-habits of the heart so we can journey together as relational people? The second part of this book focuses on counter-habits of the heart that can orient us toward mending our broken web.

5. Bellah, "Civil Religion in America."

CHAPTER THREE

Nonsingular Consciousness

Given the history of our contradictory way of relating with each other, how can we admit that our peoplehood is indeed one of a broken heart? Is there any way we can move toward a more equal and reciprocal way of relating with each other and away from our habitual adversarial fashion that we have become so accustomed to? In other words, can we move toward a kinder way and away from a cruel way of meeting each other?

As I earlier observed, Martin Buber is known for proposing two fundamentally different ways of relating to each other: One is an "I-It" way, based on objectifying and controlling the person we meet. The other is an "I-Thou" approach, which is a mutually and respectfully reciprocal way of relating that offers a degree of harmony and clarity about our societal life. Our interactions have largely been one dimensional in the "I-It" mode of relating. When we say that we meet each other oppositionally, we mean meeting people as an object, not a person with dignity, deserving of respect and reciprocity. However, the reality of our peoplehood is more complex. While the objectified separation of people is real and hurtful in our history, an oppositional relationship also produces a way we can identify and represent ourselves to others. It provides one way we can claim our own unique identity on our own terms. When we are interpreted through somebody else's terms, by opposing those terms we "object" to and relate with them as we see ourselves, not merely by the way we are seen.

While Buber's approach to relationships and communication is insightful, we need to dig deeper into the historical and societal meanings of our relationships and communications. Indeed, we are more than the binary I-It or I-Thou. There is an element of our relational "I-Thou" peoplehood even in the midst of estrangement and invisibility. When we object to being seen only on another's terms, we are saying that within the "It" is a "Thou." By this I am saying that we are relational and plural to the core. We are a people who negotiate differences and separation. We are stuck with each other. We are "we." We are not a collection of separate people. "One" does not mean "same." It means one people who relate with others across differences however equal or unequal at any given time.

Why is it so hard for us to meet our neighbors for who they truly are, on their own terms, reciprocally, instead of assuming to know who they are? I was told so many times, "I have always seen you as one of us. You are no different from us." These are the words I often heard when I was a member of an "encounter group," a life-sharing group, when I was a seminary student back in the sixties. Similar words have been spoken to me by my white friends even recently. Years ago, and lately when I heard these words, I was the only person of color when these words were spoken. Back in my earlier years I did not have the language to protest these comments and to express my own self-understanding to my friends, to say to them who I was and am as a person of color who was formed in another country, culture, and history. The words for what those comments meant then, and now, do have a language attached to them: they mean to be labeled as an "honorary white." I was, and still am to some degree, seen and treated as an honorary white by some friends and by others who only see me through their understanding of who I am without hearing my story. This happens even with their good intensions. My self-representation as a person of Japanese descent is not necessarily visible in the group of particularly all-white people. My identity, my worldview, my value orientations, my struggles get dismissed in what appear to be friendly comments. "Honorary white" is a way for the dominant society to maintain their racial status quo of superiority in terms of an "I-It" posture of relating that pretends to be "I-Thou." The term is used in a nonthreatening "kindly" way and yet it becomes a "cruel" gesture to those who are not white.

Those of us who are multilingual and multicultural have experienced how difficult it is to communicate the subtlety of meaning across language and cultural differences. We experience how hard is it to listen to a story spoken in a different language literally and figuratively. Unwittingly we are who we are, people who speak and communicate in multiple languages and sensitivities depending on whom we relate with and how we relate. We are already multilingual and multi-conscious in this sense. We also know that it is truly difficult to admit that we are people of more than one way of meeting each other. The reality of the majority consciousness is that one does not acknowledge this nonsingular reality of people in our midst. There is a reluctance on the part of the majority to admit this multilingual, multicultural consciousness, or nonsingular reality. The singular consciousness majority continues to insist that "We the People" communicate in their singular mode of relating. The danger of this singular consciousness posture is that it carries with it the assumed optimistic worldview that screens and filters out the stories of strangers with their own multiple, or nonsingular consciousness and sensitivity to pathos.

When I talk about multicultural, or nonsingular, consciousness, I am talking about a rare art of listening, speaking, and relating that is different from our familiar way of listening and speaking. The art of listening to another person's story through a multiple, nonsingular consciousness lens and sensitivity involves behavioral changes that require our intentional commitment. It cannot be accomplished overnight. It is a lifelong commitment if we ever decide to consider such a conversion of our way of being with each other. Because of this we might continue to insist on communicating in our familiar language and our familiar one-dimensional fashion. To communicate in a different way that is more reciprocally unfamiliar will involve the difficult way of choice and learning. We actually can choose, if we will, what we pay attention to, and to what we are willing to invest our lives.

We are inclined to listen to and speak a familiar language. We can continue to relegate the unfamiliar others to a peripheral corner of our own lives. This will be a tempting default choice in our culture of hyper-individualism, where personal freedom rules. For people of color, we don't have the luxury of doing so. Racial differences are too critical and ever present in every aspect of our lives. We don't have a freedom of choice not to live with people of different perspectives day in and day out. We people of color have to develop the way of hearing the language of the dominant race communities in order to communicate with them. At the same time, we also speak our own languages within our own communities to express who we are.

There is a perception gap for those who live without choice and those who can live with choice in how we negotiate our differences in relating with each other. The question of whether and how "race matters" in these negotiations depends upon one's life location. We listen to the matters of race from the particular life location we find ourselves in. For the majority, to listen to an unfamiliar voice is a matter of choice. While this is the case, the often unacknowledged truth is that one's decision to invest or not to invest one's attention to an unfamiliar voice on race or any other difference will have consequences in the world of fragmentation and polarization. The way we relate with our neighbor matters. It makes all the difference about how we chart our future. Will we journey together in a more cooperative fashion, or will we continue to live separately with growing animosity and suspicion? How we treat the question of our relatedness and differences, particularly race, is not a mere casual choice. It is the choice that affects us all. If we want to become a more equal and reciprocal people, as I trust we do, I contend this will involve everyone nurturing nonsingular consciousness for the sake of our future as "We the People." I know this is perhaps a hope-against-hope vision, but it is at least an honest aspirational goal.

NONSINGULAR CONSCIOUSNESS: SPIRITUAL STRIVINGS

Nurturing nonsingular consciousness is a spiritual striving. It is spiritual because as we attempt to know others through a nonsingular lens, we really endeavor to know ourselves, particularly when we begin to realize our limitations in how we know others.

W. E. B. Du Bois alludes to this spiritual striving when he talks about the "double consciousness" of African Americans.

> [Double consciousness arises from] a sense of always looking at one's self through the eyes of others, of measuring one's soul by the tape of a world that looks on in amused contempt and pity . . . One ever feels his twoness,—an American, a Negro; two souls, two thoughts, two unreconciled strivings; two warring ideals in one dark body, whose dogged strength alone keeps it from being torn asunder. The History of the American Negro is the history of this striving—this longing to attain self-conscious manhood, to merge his double self into a better and truer self. He simply wishes to make it possible for a man to be both a Negro and an American. Without being cursed and spit upon by his fellows, without having the doors of Opportunity closed roughly in his face.[1]

"Double consciousness" according to Du Bois is a "striving" of African Americans that can be understood as a "spiritual striving." This is so because it is a way of communicating who they are by truly representing themselves

1. Du Bois, *Soul of Black Folk*, 1–2.

to those who are the members of the racially dominant group who have their own perceptions and definitions of African Americans. African Americans in their longing to be "We the People" have developed double consciousness. This insight of Du Bois also speaks of the experiences of other people of color as well. Double consciousness, or nonsingular consciousness, is more than identity consciousness. It is more than the longing for structural change. It is a spiritual striving because it speaks to the relational reality of the peoplehood called Americans. It reveals both American potentials and limitations. Nonsingular consciousness is the reality of who we really are, a reality that is not recognized by the term "us"—except in some segments of brokenhearted communities. The "people of contradictions" have collectively failed to admit the presence of our common and "unreconciled" strivings toward nurturing the kind of nonsingular consciousness in the majority culture, a multiple consciousness that already exists in African Americans' and other people of colors' lives.

VEIL OF RESISTANCE

The contradictions embedded in American peoplehood stem from the misapprehension of our neighbors that disrespects their human dignity and worth, resulting in a tragic inequality of life and opportunities. Our neighbors are viewed as those who are worth less, deserving of less, defined as "less than" the majority people. As such, they are objectified and commodified beings of the "I-It" mentality Martin Buber describes. This posture toward others, particularly racialized "different" neighbors, is the basic cause of the brokenness of our relationships. This is the root of our broken peoplehood and the bedrock of our contradictions in history. The originating declarations that were meant to help a new nation become independent of life under the domination of another nation morphed into the freedom and right to devalue people designated as strangers within our own midst. This "less than" attitude of the majority people toward the disfranchised people has shaped the posture of powerless people's resistance responses toward them. Du Bois introduced the term "veil" to explain the African Americans' resistance to the majority race culture:

> In those somber forests of his striving his own soul rose before him, and he saw himself, dark as through a veil; and yet he saw in himself some faint revelation of his power, of his mission.[2]

The "veil" is what Du Bois terms "double consciousness" that African Americans inherently possess. It is a "sense of always looking at oneself through the eyes of others, of measuring one's soul by the tape of a world that looks on in amused contempt and pity."[3] And yet the veil is also the determination to affirm one's own dignity and worth even in the midst of a world that "looks on in amused contempt and pity." The veil is the reality of African Americans separated from the white communities. At the same time, it brings African Americans together. Du Bois sees the veil as a contradiction that reveals white communities' inability to come together with African American communities on a coequal footing. The veil is a way of distinguishing African Americans from the white communities without denying their common humanity.

"SEPARATE AND UNEQUAL" AMIDST "SEPARATE AND EQUAL"

The primary reason that we, people of color, measure our own soul "through the eyes of others" for the purpose of representing who we are "without being cursed and spit upon by" people of the majority race is to avoid isolation. Whereas for the racially majority people, nonsingular race consciousness is difficult to comprehend, let alone embrace because it exists outside of their familiar experience. Furthermore, the white majority risks becoming isolated from their fellow majority citizens by developing a double consciousness. Yet risking this isolation and plunging into a double self is a critical necessity for "meeting" unfamiliar people and trying to relate across differences, especially racial divisions. Reweaving the web of all people, or the rebirth of "We the People," will arise out of embracing nonsingular selves together. We can affirm this where we find it already existing in some aspects of our peoplehood.

Through a majority culture's willingness to receive the worldviews of their unfamiliar neighbors, a new peoplehood might come into being. Perhaps this new peoplehood is a pipe dream. It will depend upon members

2. Du Bois, *Soul of Black Folks*, 1–2.

3. Du Bois, *Soul of Black Folks*, 197.

of the majority racial group choosing to relinquish their singular race consciousness and self-identity and joining others in a multiple conscious way of living. People of color who already live with a double consciousness may open a way into this shared future. One can hope against hope for this spiritual opening.

What would motivate people of a singular race consciousness to embrace a multiple consciousness when the motivation is a matter of choice? Reawakening peoplehood must begin with admitting together our peoplehood is "separate and unequal," as the Kerner Commission named our reality. Or, as I have been saying, our history is that of a people of contradictions. To admit this would at the same time be an acknowledgment of an alternate possibility of a peoplehood—separate, yes, but at the same time equal. "Equality" does not only mean equal opportunity as conventionally understood. Equality means the admission of the presence of nonsingular ways of knowing and living amid a history that pressures us to be the "same." But homogenizing doesn't work! The history of contradictions cannot be erased. Yet in the presence of contradictions, we can also witness the alternate and plural ways some of us live our lives. Do we need to continue to live with the illusion of sameness as a people? Or can we glimpse that we live diverse and multiple ways of viewing life, including the ways that are often contrary to what is familiar to the majority? I would submit that this multiple and diverse viewing of life is a more accurate meaning of *e pluribus unum*, a reading that recognizes the journey of a broken heart.

How do we acknowledge the presence of *unum* in the midst of *pluribus*? Writer and civil rights activist Audrey Lorde points out that "one cannot dismantle the master's house with the master's tool."[4] We need to have recourse to a different "tool," or a different way of understanding what it means to belong together. Nonsingular consciousness is such a tool. This tool also means that we need a fresh paradigm for approaching the subject of peoplehood. We need the new paradigm of "out of many, we." This would be a fresh understanding in a world dominated by the existing paradigm where the majority people long for a homogeneous future represented by a harmonious "out of many, one." A new paradigm recognizes that the "One people" is actually the "many" or "We." Nonsingular consciousness is the tool for building the "We" "out of many." Nonsingular consciousness is the different tool Lorde refers to when she says, "one cannot dismantle the master's house with the master's tool." We need a different tool in order to own

4. Lorde, *Sister Outsider*, 110–14.

and internalize in our deepest beings what it means both collectively and personally a "we" united together in our history. The cultivation of nonsingular consciousness is a critical and powerful tool that is necessary for building a new paradigm of "we." This is particularly true for race relations.

For people of color and other minoritized groups, we need the means to represent ourselves as we truly see ourselves. This is difficult! Old habits and perceptions do not change easily or quickly. For people of color, we find ourselves "always looking at ourselves through the eyes of others." An integration of "a better and truer self" does not emerge easily. For one thing, the alternative outlook of life fed by a nonsingular consciousness and defiant hope arises out of the persistent pathos of life, which is seldomly recognized and scarcely appreciated. And yet, for people of color, we are used to living with the constant negation of who we are, separated, invisible, reduced to being "nobody." Nonsingular consciousness is a matter of acknowledging the status of "separate and unequal" in order to embrace the potentiality of becoming "separate and equal." Reweaving the fabric of peoplehood requires the nurturing of nonsingular race consciousness on the part of those who have lived with a taken-for-granted singular consciousness for so long. Singular consciousness is the "master's tool" that makes anyone who does not fit the roadmap of this consciousness invisible and irrelevant. Nonsingular consciousness is a different tool for building a new home for us all.

THE DIFFICULT CHALLENGE OF RACIAL TRANSFORMATION

A recent example of nonsingular consciousness is the life story of Rachel Dolezal, a controversial figure who now goes by the Nigerian name Nkechi Amare Diallo. Her life illuminates the complicated and controversial endeavor of acquiring nonsingular consciousness as a person of the racially dominant society. She is a white woman by birth who understood and claimed herself to be a black woman. As a result, she has been accused of being a con artist for concealing her biological white origin while she claimed her black identity. The accusations came both from whites and people of color, particularly African Americans. Eventually she did acknowledge her white birth identity, in her book *In Full Color*. When a white interviewer asked in a popular morning TV program, "When did you start deceiving people?" Dolezal would not concede she had done so. "I do take exception to that, because it's a little more complex than me identifying as black, or answering a question, 'Are you black or white?' . . . Well, I definitely am not white. Nothing about being white describes who I am."[5]

Dolezal has been accused of being a liar about her racial identity by African Americans. Dorothy Webster of the Spokane NAACP said, "The issue for me has been the deception, the lie, portraying herself as someone she isn't."[6] Dolezal does not accept the accusation. She has objected by saying, "As much as this discussion has somewhat been at my expense recently, and in a very sort of viciously inhumane way come out of the woodwork, the discussion is really about what it is to be human." She went on to say, "I hope that can drive at the core of definitions of race, ethnicity, culture, self-determination, personal agency and, ultimately empowerment."[7] Author and columnist Tamara Winfrey Harris made this statement when Rachel Dolezal became news: "I will accept Ms. Dolezal as black like me only when society can accept me as a white like her."[8] These comments help us understand some of the main difficulty people have in comprehending racial double consciousness. It also poses another curious question: Can one change racial identity?

Whites who "choose" to embrace double consciousness risk being placed in a liminal racial location and identity that has not been sufficiently explored or understood in race conversations. These whites are often treated with suspicion or scorn. A "con artist," a "pretender." An appropriationist. These labels reveal the deeply assumed notion that race is something fixed and permanent, for all people. Race is assumed to be something that is stable and "reliable," and therefore predictable. These understandings of race keep people "in their place," leaving no room for nuance, gradation, or change in ones' self-perception and representation. Such a rigid reading of race excludes any understanding of the lived experience of what might be called a "fluidity" of race; an understanding that might acknowledge a genuine desire on the part of a racially majority person to "meet" and "relate" with people of color.

The conversations about Dolezal are predominantly cast as a subject dealing with "transracial identity." Dolezal described herself as transracial: "Well, I definitely am not white. Nothing about being white describes who

5. Du Bois, *Soul of Black Folk*, 1–2.

6. Webster, "Rachel Dolezal."

7. Kim, "Rachel Dolezal Breaks Her Silence."

8. Webster, "Rachel Dolezal."

I am."[9] The conversation seems to be cast in terms of race being that of the question of racial "identity." While Dolezal may or may not articulate how race is presented in conversations, I find it helpful to point out how her frame of reference includes the communities to which she relates, and to which she is committed. She chose the primary community she identifies with, the African American, and emphasizes her relationship to that community and her way of being a member of that community. Her "personal identity" is a referential piece in talking about her choice of that community and how she sees herself in it by moving away from the white community of her original racial family. In other words, I see the primary factor of the Dolezal matter being how she moved away from a singular consciousness that formed her into being white to the formational change of being a member of a different racial and familial community. It is also interesting to wonder if, in the process, she also moved away from the ideal of an individual self, toward a more relational experience of selfhood.

One can ask, how did Dolezal undergo her formational shift? Did she see herself as black throughout her process, or was it a gradual transformation? Did she abandon her original formation in her white family in order to become a member of the black community? What were the limitations she experienced in doing so? What "tools" did she employ in redefining her unconventional and controversial shift of relationships that led her to move away from the dominant power group to a marginal racial group and her embracing the black community? That she did undergo a transformational life experience is clear. This was not simply an identity change, even though identity played its own role. She was undergoing a transformation, not only in personal terms, but in community relationships, with its accompanying shift in values and life outlook. She might not have been accurate, or even adequate in terms of describing the meaning of her transformation. As I listen to her story, I wonder if she had an adequate language or frame of reference to fully explain to others her experience. My observation of her life focuses on these issues and questions. The "non-master's tool," nonsingular consciousness, I employ for my inquiry can be further understood as "the tool of transformation." This tool is not founded upon a negotiated identity but relies on community relatedness. As she became changed through these relationships, she found herself in a new and unfamiliar place as she tried to prove her reformed place in American peoplehood.

9. Webster, "Rachel Dolezal."

The Dolezal case opens up the question of what race means in a more complex fashion today. The taken-for-granted way the subject of race for the Dolezal discourse is framed is that of identity: "The reason that her story is so fascinating to me is that it exposes in a disquieting way that our race is viewed as performance, that, despite the stark differences in how our races are perceived and privileged (or not) by others, they are all predicated on a myth that the differences are intrinsic and intrinsically perceptible," says Steven W. Thrasher, a columnist for *The Guardian*.[10] The history of race discourse suggests that visible "perceptions" often drive race identity differences, particularly from both the perspectives of the racially dominant group of people as well as persons of color. "Are you a con artist?" Dolezal was asked in an interview. The hidden assumption behind that question is that she does not look black. She hid her white background. The framework for questioning Dolezal is racial identity. Thus, the conversation of race moves in the direction of distinctness of identity and the impossibility of change. Historically the matter of race has been discussed in terms of identity. While this has been appropriate for discussing the subject of racism, it is also limited.

There is another layer that lies below how Dolezal "looks" in the eye of the public. The accusation of Dolezal for being a racial impersonator is also related to the history of whites who appropriated black identity and appearance when it was useful to them, mainly for entertainment, not for an expression of a living transformation. Until recently this "switching" has not been questioned. Yet the prevailing assumption of our society is that if you are white, casting off one's racial location of whiteness for another racial category is an appropriation, stealing, not being honest about one's given race identity. People of color cannot do this kind of exchange, and therefore have no choice but to live by the racial identity assigned to them. But Rod Dreher in *The American Conservative* cautions the hypocrisy of liberals "for accepting transgendered Caitlyn Jenner as a woman, but not Ms. Dolezal as black. . . . So, to recap, if Rachel Dolezal says she is a man, we must agree, on pain of being publicly censured. But if Rachel Dolezal says she is black, it is fair game to challenge her claim."[11] My question is, why does race provoke such polarizing responses whereas other controversial subjects such as gender, sexuality, cultural, and spiritual identities do not, at least not to the same extent?

10. Perez-Pena, "Black or White?"

11. Dreher, "Call Me Rosa Parks."

An extreme and absurd reading of race identity is the infamous "one drop of blood" theory that says legally a person is black if there is "one drop" of blood that can be traced biologically to black ancestry, no matter how white the person "appears." The hidden assumption of the "one drop of blood" theory is that a black person is biologically different, and furthermore "subhuman" and "inferior" in the eye of the racially majority population. In this view, a black person's identity is fixed and does not change. This "fixed" racial identity seems to be attributed to all racially classified individuals as well, while the value of white identity is valued as superior.

At the heart of the Dolezal controversy is the annoyance on the part of African Americans and others who disparage her is that she cannot own the pathos of their race history since she did not carry the historical weight of African Americans. For many whites, she is "seen" as a plain liar or pretender who takes advantage of a fashionable cause of racial justice today. For some African Americans she is a con artist. What is missing in this controversy is the question of inherently unstable and nomadic nonsingular racial identity. I will address this subject in the chapter 5, "The Illusion of Precision," for understanding race. Furthermore, the question of why race matters is not solely the issue of racial identity, it is the issue of differences of power and value, where some people are treated as human beings and others as subhumans. The discussion of racial identity as exemplified in the Rachael Dolezal case is focused on what is perceived as racial identities.

When we look at race through the framework of the tool of transformation, where the focus is on communal relations and internal value shifts, additional factors begin to come into focus. The accent becomes the "relationship" of people across whatever the lines of difference. The key question of race from this angle of discussion becomes: Can a person who has been *formed white* culturally and personally be *reformed culturally* and relationally as "black," and be accepted as a way we live together? I believe Rachael Dolezal attempted this kind of transformation and has paid a tremendous price for her efforts. She left the realm of the familiar singular white consciousness and moved into the realm of nonsingular black consciousness in order to relate with black people and communities. Whether she *wanted* to be black rather than white is not certain from her explanation. "Well, I definitely am not white. Nothing about being white describes who I am," she said. Yet, whatever happened in her shift, transformation was not able to be reversed in her case and cannot be reversed if one fully makes this transition. In her process of transformation, she has become alienated from many in the white community as well as from many African Americans. What has she learned from this process of change? What is the primary community of her belonging today? What does it mean as a person who was formed as white to be transformed toward becoming black? These questions arise out of looking at race from the angle of formation and transformation, in addition to that of identity.

I am suggesting we rotate the kaleidoscope to reveal a different configuration to talk about the subject of race in the Dolezal case. We might see a different frame of reference, one that speaks to a relational and transformational way of interpreting racial dynamics. Racial injustices and racism seen within this framework can give depth and meaning to the standard racial identity methodology for talking about race. The question of peoplehood from this perspective is dependent upon how to meet people across what alienates one from another. If one dares to cross the perceived racial divide, and in doing so becomes accused of being a con artist and a fake, how can one genuinely attempt to relate with those who are unfamiliar and different?[12] Dolezal notes: "As we grow and evolve, we should keep in mind that a single person's identity, or even the identity of a group of people, isn't the root problem when it comes to race. How people identify themselves along the racial spectrum and how they are treated based on that identification are only symptomatic of the real problem [of] racism."[13] Dolezal seems to understand that our human identity is relational to its core, that a full, direct, and mutual encounter between and among people in the midst of whatever separates and estranges us is the foundation of our life together. As long as difference is assumed solely on the basis of separate identities, without acknowledging both our relatedness *and* separation, we will continue to stay locked within the wall of rigid difference and distance that only perpetuates estrangement. The way of approaching the subject of race based on the "relational" dimensions of race opens up previous identity theories and politics for fresh possibilities of understandings.

On the subject of peoplehood, when we ask what can hold people together, this relational dimension of race is significant. It shifts the matter of "transformation" and change in the ways we relate with each other away from the perceived identity or "transracialism" problematics of race to new relational ways of seeing and understanding. It is significant that what matters for race theory is the very real process of one's life formation

12. Tuvel, "In Defense of Transracialism."

13. Dolezal, *In Full Color*, 276.

and reformation in relationship with diverse people. This shift is necessary in order to share life together with those who are "We." And it is important to emphasize that the "We" includes those whose lives have long been neglected and unjustly treated as a result of our false perceptions of the web of peoplehood. The question is not about changing one's fixed racial identity, it is about how we become transformed through relationships. And, of course, this is where power dynamics and values come critically into play.

CAN WE "KNOW" ANOTHER PERSON?

Nonsingular consciousness goes beyond what Du Bois talked about in "double consciousness." His focus was on the double consciousness that African Americans developed as a way to negotiate white dominance. I am using the term to include other racialized experiences of negotiating across multiple communities of difference. Nonsingular consciousness in this regard is acknowledging the status of "separate and unequal" in our "Weness," and our yearning for becoming a "separate and equal peoplehood." Transformation is a necessary way of knowing a person and community who are our neighbors but who have become strangers. But can we really know our neighbors? How can a stranger become somebody to us instead of being seen as a nobody so that we can meet mutually? What are the limits of relating with a stranger who is our neighbor? Dealing with limitations is also at the heart of cultivating nonsingular consciousness.

My response to this question of limitations is simple but also complex. We need to listen to unfamiliar voices *on their own terms* for reawakening our peoplehood, to acknowledge the presence of counter-habits of the heart revealed in the brokenness of our communal heart. By listening to the voices of a "nobody" on their own terms, we come to know their presence in our midst and who they are. But I would state that listening is an incredibly difficult task because our own limitations get in the way of hearing these other voices.

Rachael Dolezal struggled to be heard. I am not sure whether she was able to be heard by the way she attempted to explain who she was. She said, "For most, Blackness comprises much more than one's physical appearance. It's the culture you inhabit and the experiences you've lived. It's philosophical, emotional, even spiritual."[14] Does she succeed in communicating how she experienced her change in relating with her original white family

14. Dolezal, *In Full Color*, 3.

and community of white people? How about her relationship to the family, friends, and community of black people? How does she explain what it is to live "in between" the worlds of white and black groups? What attracted her to black communities in the first place? What does she mean when she says she is black? And why did she not originally acknowledge her relations with her white family and friends? What does it mean to move away from the life of singular consciousness to the "veiled" consciousness that Du Bois mentions? How does she find herself changed or transformed as a person? And what does she see as the kaleidoscopic images change endlessly by rotating the fragments of her life? These questions become guideposts to how we come to know another person or a group of people, particularly across the line of difference through the frame of relationships.

Anthropologists Clifford Geertz and Victor Turner began the conversation about living "in between" spaces. Later, anthropologist Ruth Behar continued this inquiry. These researchers became curious about people who are caught between one experience of formation and another form of formation, whether by necessity or by choice. They pursued the question: How can one communicate the state of in-betweenness, a liminal space of life, to those for whom it is a totally unfamiliar experience? How can you explain in a brief conversation the transformation that occurs over the course of a lifetime? You can't.[15] This is the kaleidoscopic dilemma in addressing the subject of race. We are unstable, uncertain, ambiguous, and disorienting beings and we continue to try to be stable, certain, and convinced of who we are. Is it possible to be changed and transformed to something new and unexpected from this familiar and stable notion of self? It seems like an almost insurmountable venture. No wonder Dolezal had difficulty explaining herself "in a brief conversation on the street [something] that occurred over the course of a lifetime."[16] What does it mean to "know" a person even with the cultivation of a nonsingular consciousness and the transformation of one's self?

Anthropologist Ruth Behar's experience of interviewing Esperanza for her research gives us some insights about the difficulty of "knowing" someone with radically different life experiences. Her aim for her research appears simple enough at first glance: to tell the life story of "Esperanza," a Mexican village peddler. As a Cuban American researcher Behar thought this would be simple enough and a straightforward endeavor. But she found

15. Dolezal, *In Full Color*, 4.

16. Dolezal, *In Full Color*, 4.

this not to be the case at all. Her conclusion says that the best one can do to "meet" another person, especially across the cultural and racial divide, is to "translate" that person in light of one's own cultural and racial formation. In other words, the goal to "understand" is illusive, so the researcher cannot fully "understand" or "represent" that person.

Esperanza is poor, but somehow trying to be independent of her abusive husband. She is alienated from her neighbors for her outspoken arrogance and at times she is even called a "witch." She does not fit the stereotypical Mexican woman, passive and self-abnegating. She is self-sufficient. She expresses her rage against abusive men. Behar is Cuban-born and of European-Jewish descent. She emigrated to the US at age six. In the course of interviewing Esperanza over several years, she begins to see the difference and distance in social, cultural, and racial locations between herself and Esperanza. Behar is a *gringa*: white, middle-class, living comfortably in the US. "What does it mean that Esperanza's historian can cross the border with me . . . but that Esperanza herself cannot . . . ?"[17] A revealing question! Esperanza's odyssey forces Behar to examine physical borders, margins, and separations. Behar's own self-involved scrutiny of her own life ambitions, her own career path and privilege, ends up undermining her very pursuit of the life story of Esperanza. Behar recognizes that what she does in her anthropological research is at best to "translate" Esperanza and her story. She can neither "represent" Esperanza nor "grasp" her. There is always the unknown and in truth, the unknowable, in relating with another person, especially over cultural and racial divides. Furthermore, as a cultural anthropologist Behar came to acknowledge that she is a "vulnerable observer" who cannot to be fully detached from the person who is the subject of her research. She is "involved" in the life of the subject under study.

In a similar fashion becoming consciously nonsingular in race relationship is not merely making a practical choice of "knowing" people of another race. It is to enter into relationship with those who have been seen as "different" and "less than." It means becoming "involved." Moreover, it means to become honest about one's own racial formation and to become "vulnerable." It really means to acknowledge one's own life as a "homeland" of stored memory and pain.[18] In meeting others, we can only *translate* that person. We cannot fully "know" that person or "represent" that person in the way they would choose to represent themself. Because of this we also

17. Behar, *Translated Woman*, 21.

18. DeVault, "Book Review."

learn to see ourselves, our own limitations to understand and relate with another person. In the words of pastoral theologian Sharon Thornton, "Understanding ourselves through the other's eyes helps all of us discover more fully what it means to address brokenness in our common life."[19] Entering into relationships where we are not the originators of another's story, or perhaps even our own, we encounter the "themes of difference found in places of dislocation and displacement."[20] From centers of displacement we meet another, be it an individual or a community of people; we witness the "brokenness" of relationships.

"Any man's death diminishes me, because I am involved in mankind," as poet John Donne acknowledges.[21] Relationship is the foundation of our being. If you touch one part of the human web, the whole web trembles. Given this, the reawakening of peoplehood is only realizable when we know that we are alienated from one another all along and that we need a way of re-establishing a web of all people. The rebirth of peoplehood, or a reweaving of the societal fabric, will emerge out of this realization. Once again, in the words of Frederick Buechner, "The paradox is that part of what binds us closer together as human beings and makes it true that no man is an island is the knowledge that in another way every man is an island."[22] When one group of people suffers, the whole web of peoplehood suffers. "Any one's death diminishes me, because I am who I am because I am a member of humankind. And therefore, never send to know for whom the bell tolls; it tolls for thee."

Practicing this "paradoxical" reality of "I-Thou" is the way to the reawaken our peoplehood made up of "We the People." This means owning the reality of our brokenness as the foundation of "We the People." This means accepting our brokenness as that which can bring us together as "We." Owning the fracture at the center of our life together is a way of beginning to dismantle "the master's house" by abandoning the master's tools. The honest acknowledgment of broken peoplehood goes hand in hand with the search for a non-master tool that will take us out of the familiar master's house toward our new peoplehood.

Again, as Martin Luther King Jr. reminds us, "People fail to get along because they fear each other; they fear each other because they don't know

19. Thornton, "Honoring Rising Voices."

20. Thornton, "Honoring Rising Voices."

21. Donne, *Complete Poetry and Selected Prose*, 403.

22. Buechner, *Hungering Dark*, 47.

each other; they don't know each other because they have not communicated with each other."[23] But more than that, in our current situation we are an island to each other. In this fundamental way, we are strangers to each other. This suggests to us why we don't communicate with those who are different and important for our relationships. The broken reality of "We" "is a way of speaking about the indwelling presence of others in our own concrete reality and of our presence in others," as Archie Smith Jr. says.[24] We need to trust other people's experiences as they relate them, particularly the majority people need to trust the previously silenced voices. Both the majority and minoritized voices need to participate in the relational exchange. The bond needed for the rebirth of peoplehood means we are indeed all "relational selves." This means that America can never be a "people" unless we recognize that we all need to acknowledge in our heads and feel in our hearts the lives of people who do not share our own familiar life experiences. We all need to recognize the experiences of kindness as well as cruelty, particularly in racial and other differences, as our own. We are Americans because we indeed are a people of various life outlooks, especially the separate outlooks of unfamiliar people in our own lives.

We are Americans even as we have not communicated with each other. The tool of nonsingular transformation based on a relational understanding of peoplehood is a paradigm of paradox that says that one's well-being is dependent upon recognizing the brokenness of "We the People." This recognition is the reason that "we need each other greatly you and I, more than much of the time we dare to imagine, more than most of the time we dare to admit."[25] *Unum*, "living together," indeed comes out of *pluribus*, the reality of broken and estranged state in which we all have lived for so long in history. The web of life, that "no one is an island," is not realized by mere wishing or longing for it, collectively or individually. The web of life, the "relational life," is realized out of the brutally honest acknowledgment that we have indeed been islands unto ourselves all along. Only when we know our broken state in history, and now, can we begin to know that we need to reach out to people, especially the unknown and stranger, because we do not, and cannot, live alone. The web of life grows out of our deficits, our brokenness of relationships, not out of our simple desire to be with others. Alexis de Tocqueville named this alienated state of peoplehood in the US

23. King Jr., *Papers*, 555.

24. Smith Jr., *Relational Self*, 51.

25. Buechner, *Hungering Dark*, 47.

"the tyranny of the majority."[26] This is also the tyranny of individualism that perpetuates one's well-being by silencing the voices of others. It is a distorted reading of the sanctity of freedom, a freedom that serves some while ignoring others—people at the edge. For the renewal of peoplehood, nurturing nonsingular consciousness, or multiple consciousness, is needed, for it gives us an opportunity to "hear" the unfamiliar voices, particularly those at the edge. This is so in order to seek healing of our broken yet beloved dream of America.

26. Tocqueville, *Democracy in America*, 235–40.

CHAPTER FOUR

Defiant Hope

I will light a candle; hope it blossoms into a steady flame of peace and say these words aloud: "We are included. We belong. We are here." For, just like you—entitled by birthright, we have a place in this world too.[27]

THESE ARE THE WORDS of Unitarian Universalist Minister Carol Thomas Cissel in "Being Black in America." Can these words be said by the whole "We the People" who gather out of many diverse life experiences? Can hope for "We are included. We belong. We are here." be sustained even in the midst of a hopelessness for its realization? This is the question of this chapter.

"Every person is a piece of the continent, A part of the main. . . . The death of every person diminishes the whole peoplehood."[28] The relational potential of peoplehood, "I-Thou," is not a static descriptive statement of who we are. It is a powerful driving force for all the people who yearn to become and belong together. Throughout our history we have named our yearning *e pluribus unum*. Its origin is not known precisely. But ancient Greek philosopher Heraclitus talked about "the one is made up of all things, and all things issue from one." It is translated to mean "Out of many, one" or "One from many." It thus became the great seal of our nation. This motto also points to the transitory and aspirational character of our peoplehood, "in order to form a more perfect Union." We are people who are on the way,

27. Cissel, in Peters, "Being Black in America."

28. Donne, paraphrased from his poem, "No Man Is an Island."

coming from "many" moving toward "We," not a homogenized "One." The Declaration of Independence says:

> When in the Course of human Events, it becomes necessary for one People to dissolve the Political Bands which have connected them with another, and to assume among the Powers of the Earth, the separate and equal station to which the Laws of Nature and of Nature's God entitle them, a decent Respect to the Opinions of Mankind requires that they should declare the causes which impel them to the Separation.

This is a statement of a particular understanding of hope. It is an aspirational view of who we are that is "not yet." The "not yet" points to the contradictions inherent in our relationships. We are "being separated" and not yet together.

The reality of these contradictions has given rise to another version of hope. It is a hope that appears among the people who have experienced decades of "not yet" through centuries of despair, dehumanization, tragedy and, yes, hopelessness. The not yet carries the hint of "and yet," which gives rise to a defiant hope, or "hope against hope" that the "yet" will become real. This hope is common among people of color along with others who are located at the edge of our society. Hope against hope motivates us to see amidst the experiences of sufferings and tragedy the presence of equality, liberty, and justice no matter how difficult they may be to reach, even if these "unalienable rights" may not ever be realized. It is hope that is tasted in the marrow of hardship. While we are separate we know we are equal. This hope against hope can be "here and now" even though "not here and not yet."

Aspirational hope ("in order to form a more perfect Union") and defiant hope both exist side by side in our history. Sometimes they intersect with each other, most often they don't. Mostly aspirational hope is the public vision we project into the future, whereas defiant hope points to the engine, the motivation that drives us with determination to the as-yet-unfulfilled vision for our days ahead. In both views hope is a treacherous venture. They both merit self-determination and commitment. Hope against hope begs for self-sacrificing actions that bring changes. Changes that arise out of imagining and striving for what we have yet to see possible. Each understanding of hope speaks to a sense of purpose, and each involves a journey, albeit journeys that involve different paths to negotiate.

In our history of individualism, we have adopted a particular posture to face an unknown future. The assumed posture is one of confidence wrapped in unfurling optimism, even amid inevitable intrusions of tragedy and despair. Reinhold Niebuhr understood this optimism as the "single article of faith that has given diverse forms of modern culture the unity of a shared belief."[29] What is shared among people is that whenever a particular form of government becomes destructive, people have the right to "alter or to abolish it, and to institute a new Government, laying its foundation on such principles and organizing its powers in such form, as to them shall seem most likely to affect their Safety and Happiness." Douglas John Hall calls this version of shared belief a "contradiction of experience and expectation." He observes that "our society is in a state of contradictions because its expectations and its experience no longer meet and inform each other."[30] Our future is paradigmatically anticipated in this state of contradictions.

A favorite hymn of Martin Luther King Jr. and James Baldwin intoned, "Precious Lord, take my hand. Lead me on, let me stand. I am tired, I am weak, through the night, Lead me on to the light, Precious Lord, take my hand, lead me home." This African American hymn, unlike the confidence and trust in the brightness of a redemptive future, reveals a different posture of hope, a hope steeped in defiance and a refusal to simply submit to the experiences of tragedy and affliction of a false redemptive future. The expectation of the future in this hymn arises out of the present experiences of pathos. Defiant hope says "no" to the finality of pathos in the present as well as the future. These divergent postures of hope, aspirational based on an uncritical acceptance of a redemptive future, and defiant hope rooted in pathos, often do not inform each other toward charting a shared trajectory of life. Every once in awhile they complement each other, as when MLK said: "All we say to America is this: 'Be true to what you said on paper . . .' Somewhere I read of the freedom of assembly. Somewhere I read of the freedom of speech. Somewhere I read of the freedom of the press. Somewhere I read that the greatness of America is the right to protest for right."[31]

What drives defiant hope is a stubborn vision that there can yet be some kind of congruence between experience and expectation.

29. Niebuhr, *Faith and History*, 2–4.

30. Hall, *Lighten Our Darkness*, 73.

31. King Jr., "I've Been to the Mountaintop."

TOWARD SEPARATE AND EQUAL STATIONS

The official vision of people becoming "separate and equal" leads the majority people to a taken-for-granted, upbeat posture toward the future, whereas the experiences of "separate and unequal" for other groups of people shapes a suspicious and obstinate posture. If the presence of these divergent images and visions of peoplehood is not acknowledged, we will continue to live in separate and, for all purposes, foreign worlds. Once our differences become widely entrenched, both in private and public life, we are unlikely to engage in relationships with each other. We are more likely to see those who are different as unknowable, especially those who are not our like-minded friends who share similar expectations and similar experiences. This leads to an almost intractable alienation where we become "outsiders" to one another. Those unlike us may even become an enemy for the sake of self-interest and self-preservation. These are really deviant forms of individualism, not an individualism that tries to advance "freedom" for all individuals. Our history tells us that we often resort to violence in order to settle our differences. In other words, the contradictions of expectations and experience lead to disengagement from the civic life of the whole people for the sake of attaining manageable individual expectations for those still under the illusion of "one people." This is not productive, and it isn't working. This illusion of oneness gets expressed in a dangerous form of individualism.

"A progressive union between the society of God's being and the society of God's saints" that Jonathan Edwards saw as the future of this nation gradually turned into a less explicit theological notion of self-serving optimism. Thus civil religion was born. Robert Bellah terms it the "transcendent universal religion of the nation," or "an institutionalized collection of sacred beliefs about the American nation."[32] Bellah claims that Americans largely assumed "common religious characteristics expressed through vague civil religious beliefs, symbols, and rituals that provide a religious dimension to the entirety of American life."[33] The beginning of civil religion was heavily theological and steeped in the tradition of its distinct American Christianity. It has gradually become unmoored from that origin into a unique quasi-"religion" of its own. This particular brand of religiosity continues to be the source of liberal democracy in the republic with its positivistic outlook of life.

32. Bellah et al., *Habits of the Heart*, 168 and 255.

33. Bellah et al., *Habits of the Heart*, 168 and 255.

Unlike France, where Christianity was viewed as an ally of its old political regime before the Revolution of 1789, American expressions of Christian faith in civil religion were respected and remain so as an undergirding moral value system to confront excessive individualism and materialism. Tocqueville pointed this out and it seemed to hold true, at least until recently. The religious scene has become much more diversified along with the increasing visibility and diverse voices of racial and other underrepresented groups.

The founders of the Republic tried to make sure that this nation would be an embodiment of their theological vision of the new Israel. However, it was civil religion that became the glue to hold people together. This took place as the original theological vision gradually became so diversified that it could no longer serve as the foundation of this society. Samuel Goldman critiques the current discussion of the trend toward Christian nationalism, saying we are instead moving toward small and diverse expressions of nationalism where opposing difference is the driving characteristic of our society. These local atomic communities support political projects grounded in local communities that foster narrow local interests.[34] This is nothing new: it is simply a brand of nationalism that is an extension of one form of civil religion that has been around for some time. At the same time, this brand of civil religion has become a blatant expression of highly racialized norms and values in mainly white communities. The ascendance and growing predominance of these communities tend to ignore the voices of the people who experience pathos and hopelessness and do not readily share their optimistic outlook on life.

Unlike current Christian nationalism, I contend that *Unum*, the "One," that is assumed in our national motto, is actually a gathering of people with increasingly different viewpoints, values, and life experiences that makes up the assumed "One." In other words, *Unum* in reality is "we together." Another way of saying this is, *Unum* is a peoplehood. Unfortunately, the functional language of "One" has come to take on quasi-religious and spiritual dimensions, both in the original theological language of the founders and the subsequent language of civil religion and individualism.

The notion of "faith" in our unique aspirational and redemptive notion of history, has its own theological grounding.[35] Reinhold Niebuhr prefigured Hall when he said: "The conception of a redemptive history informs

34. Goldman, *After Nationalism*.

35. Goldman, *After Nationalism*, 54.

the most diverse forms of modern culture."[36] I am saying racism rests on this faith framework. Separation and inequality continue because, and I emphasize, we trust that they will eventually be overcome in the future through our redemptive faith in history itself. The future is bright! The contradictions of our peoplehood are just different outlooks of life based on our different experiences and understandings about this nation. These contradictions that we live are consistent with faith in this positivistic history. This, then, makes our contradictions a virtue! At the same time the absence of the stories full of pathos of the neglected people provide a tragic undertow to this optimistic outlook.

In truth, it is a lack of faith that rejects the history of cruelty. The wholesale embracing of our kindness steeped in optimism obliterates the cruelty experienced by those of a different "faith," a faith rooted in a defiant hope, not redemptive history. Our contradictions point to an unawareness on the part of the majority people, or what Reinhold Niebuhr calls the irony of history, which is that the virtue of positivistic history turns out to a vice for the well-being of our whole society.

DEFIANT HOPE REVEALED

How do we undertake the art of orienting our civic heart, mind, and spirit toward relationships of mutuality and reciprocity? In other words, how can we truly become separate, related and equal? We become a "people" when we seek to be part of a whole together. This seeking has its basis in our hope for a more perfect union while acknowledging the defiant hope against hope that is a part of this seeking. Hope, in its various expressions, is what carries out the challenge, to "secure the Blessings of Liberty to ourselves and our Posterity."

We have been sustained by hope, particularly during the times of various threats to our democracy. However, the history of our peoplehood does not attest to the realization of this hope. The word "hope" that is so critical in our understanding of peoplehood has been one-sided, an aspirational hope *"to form a more perfect union . . ."* A sizeable segment of our population has lived with a different kind of hope, a defiant hope, a hope against hope.

Hope against hope speaks to a life that has been hard for so many. They have not had the luxury of simply trusting in a better life. They have

36. Niebuhr, *Faith and History*, 3.

known too much hopelessness all their lives. Thus many people have become resigned to a life of pain, poverty, inequality, and the absence of a free and bright future. Yet, they have also refused to accept what seems to be the inevitable and irredeemable despairing life. They choose to be defiant. James Baldwin's letter written to his nephew in *The Fire Next Time* talks about what fuels defiant hope. Addressing his nephew, Baldwin talks about what is at stake behind defiant hope. It will ignite the kind of hope that is needed for establishing an authentic "We, the People":

> This is the crime of which I accuse my country and my countrymen, and for which neither I nor time nor history will ever forgive them, that they have destroyed and are destroying hundreds of thousands of lives and do not know it and do not want to know it . . .[37]

He is talking to his nephew about rage that lurks in the lives of so many unheard people. This rage fuels a powerful and unexpected hope—hope against hope:

> You were born into a society which spelled out with brutal clarity, and in as many ways as possible, that you were a worthless human being. . . . But these men are your brothers—your lost, younger brothers. And if the word integration means anything, this is what it means that we, with love, shall force our brothers to see themselves as they are, to cease fleeing from reality and begin to change it. For this is your home, my friend, do not be driven from it; great men have done great things here, and will again, and we can make America what it must become. It will be hard, but you come from sturdy, peasant stock, men who picked cotton and dammed rivers and built railroads, and, in the teeth of most terrifying odds, achieved an unassailable and monumental dignity. You come from a long line of great poets since Homer. One of them said: *The very time I thought I was lost, My dungeon shook and my chains fell off.* . . . We cannot be free until they are free. God bless you, and Godspeed.[38]

In this description of what hope against hope means, Baldwin is pointing to the act of redeeming the tragic from its imprisonment within the official narrative of aspirational hope that strives toward forming "a more perfect union." For numerous voiceless people, particularly the minority race people, our history has been and continues to be tragic, not redemptive. A reading of history based on the life of pathos reveals a rage that does

37. Baldwin, *Fire Next Time*, 5–10.

38. Baldwin, *Fire Next Time*, 5.

not go away. It also reveals the source of their hope against hope. I ask, is there enough silence, a silence that might provide an opening, in our collective soul, to delve into his words, "do not be driven" from the experience of the abyss? Is there enough silence to hear the hidden hope that is there in the abyss? The rage that gives rise to a hope against hope does not belong to the voiceless alone. Even unacknowledged, it belongs to all as a festering dis-ease and a source of new peoplehood. No one can be free until all are free.

Michelle Alexander is another voice who picks up on the wisdom of James Baldwin. Are we ready to hear her words? She tells us:

> The rage may frighten us; it may remind us of riots, uprisings, and buildings aflame. We may be tempted to control it, or douse it with buckets of doubt, dismay, and disbelief. But we should do no such thing. Instead, when a young man who was born in the ghetto and who knows little of life beyond the walls of his prison cell and the invisible cage that has become his life, turns to us in bewilderment and rage, we should do nothing more than look him in the eye and tell him the truth.[39]

Defiant hope, or hope against hope, takes a variety of expressions in our racialized history. The art of *gaman* is one way Japanese Americans have expressed this defiant hope. In their experiences of concentration camps during World War II those Japanese Americans, more than two-thirds of whom were American citizens by birth, used whatever scraps they could find in the camps to make furniture and various objects of beauty. Tools, teapots, and ornamental displays are actual manifestations of the art of *gaman*, a Japanese word that means to bear the seemingly unbearable with dignity and patience. Delphine Hirasuna, the author of *The Art of Gaman*, says:

> To move on, they could not dwell on the betrayal. *Gaman* for the Nisei meant staying silent, talking up the "good times," and denying the magnitude of their loss. Facing neighbors and friends they knew before the war aroused embarrassment on both sides. The Nisei felt the tinging humiliation of knowing they had been wronged, and the white community recognized belatedly that a terrible injustice had been committed. As a result, no one talked about the camps—not in public, lest it make anyone uncomfortable, not in Japanese American homes, lest it bring on paralyzing bitterness and despair. It was only in the late 1970s—nearly thirty-five years after the closing of the camps—that the Nisei began to

39. Alexander, *New Jim Crow*, 261, and Baldwin, *Fire Next Time*, 5–10.

> allow themselves to feel their pain and demand an official apology from the government.[40]
>
> The dogged perseverance in the midst of businesses lost, personal property stolen or vandalized, lives shattered, then imprisoned in remote camps in the middle of nowhere surrounded by barbed wire and guarded by soldiers with machine guns, these Americans of Japanese descent practiced defiance through the works of art fashioning furniture from scrap lumber, weaving baskets from unraveled twine, making corsages from shells dug up from an ancient seabed. What they created is a celebration of the nobility of the human spirit in adversity.[41]
>
> We have to *gaman*—accept what is with patience and dignity. They repeated this so often, it sounded like a mantra.[42]

Japanese Americans who underwent concentration experiences demonstrated their embrace of defiant hope in the 442nd Infantry Regiment Team of the US Army during World War II. Their story, well-known among Asian American communities but seldom heard beyond them, is a noble voicing of what peoplehood means for them amidst their willingness to sacrifice their individual selves for the nation. History records this regiment as the most decorated unit for its size in US military history. The unit was created in response to the War Department's attempt to form a volunteer group of Japanese Americans for an army combat unit. The order indicated: "All cadre men must be American citizens of Japanese ancestry who have resided in the United States since birth . . . and, Officers of filed grade and captains furnished under the provisions of subparagraph a., b. and c. above will be white American citizens. Other officers will be of Japanese ancestry in so far as practicable."[43]

More than 12,000 second-generation Nisei Americans responded to the call. Many of them came from Hawaii. But what is noteworthy is that 1,500 volunteers came from incarceration camps set up for Japanese Americans. Altogether more than 800 of them lost their lives by the time the war was over, their families remained incarcerated in camps while they fought in Europe. The motto for the unit was "Go for Broke." It was their

40. Hirasuna, *Art of Gaman*, 124.

41. Hirasuna, *Art of Gaman*, front cover.

42. Hirasuna, *Art of Gaman*, 7.

43. Wakamatsu, "Origins of the 442nd Regimental Combat Team."

way of expressing defiant hope. The official history of this unit emphasizes the military awards given to it. Including the 100th Infantry Battalion, they earned over 18,000 awards, more than 4,000 Purple Hearts and 4,000 Bronze Star Medals. The tremendous sacrifice the unit members made was for the vision of an American peoplehood of equality, freedom, and justice. This vision for America was held even when it so blatantly violated the members of the unit. Their vision, supported by a spirit of *gaman*, speaks of their defiant stance of hope through their artistic expressions. Do we have an ear to hear such a story and an eye to see the art? The art of *gaman* is not just an art that belongs to Americans of Japanese descent. It is an art of all America. It cannot be genuinely appreciated until we all appreciate and embrace its underlying belief in defiant hope that belongs to us all.

DEFIANT HOPE DWELLS IN THE HEART

But where do we find the opportunities for people to appreciate the art of *gaman*? Where do we join James Baldwin in saying "we cannot be free unless they are free." As noted, we are a nation of contradictions in a society that is full of fractured and increasingly adversarial ways we relate with each other. There is less public confidence today in the promise of "one out of many." Where is the hope for the "Blessings of Liberty to ourselves and our Posterity"? How can we reweave the fabric of peoplehood when we don't trust each other, when we don't see eye to eye, when we don't want to know our neighbors whose lives are full of unresolved pain?

It is obvious that we are likely to associate with those whose lifestyles and outlooks are similar to our own rather than with strangers. But this inclination is accentuated when it comes to the matter of race. While we are more tolerant today of diversity in our schools, workplaces, and public gatherings than in the past, we are also more distanced one from another in the places we live, shop, and worship. And we are even more distanced from each other by the people we vote into public offices. So, in addition to race, we are also separated by political views and stances on sexuality, voting rights, poverty, and the ways we treat access to healthcare.

The Black Lives Matter movement, violence against Pacific Islanders and Asian Americans, and the brutal treatment of both documented and undocumented people around the southern boarder clearly point to the fissures in a society that are alarmingly evident today. We often choose not to know each other. Not only do we not know each other, at times we *don't want to know* each other. The naked truth about not knowing each other is that we shy away from the pathos of life, particularly the painful life of our neighbors. We turn toward that "officially optimistic life" we assume is the basic posture of who we are as people. As I have been emphasizing, a large segment of our population continues to live the life of pain, and yet this reality has not been acknowledged. Too often it has been dismissed as "whining" and not valued as the basic reality for so many. It cannot be said enough, we really don't know our neighbors. Then, when "things fall apart," whatever the "centers" are that we trust, they do not hold us together.

James Cone explains the difference between aspirational hope and defiant hope in his critique of Reinhold Niebuhr's understanding of black suffering. Cone contends Niebuhr "had 'eyes to see' black suffering, but I believe he lacked the 'heart to feel' it as his own."[44] The official articulation of hope as faith in redemptive history, "to form a more perfect Union," has led to an understanding of difference as "an eye to see," but it failed to engender a feeling in the heart. This incongruence is buried in the heart of our nation's optimism. This optimistic trust in the future belongs to our head, whereas the memory and rage of the painful life belongs to our heart. What is lodged in our head can be understood in a variety of ways whereas the pain that dwells in our heart stays there and does not go away. What we have in our collective heart is the accumulation of pain that has been there ever since the beginning of our nation.

The desire "to form a more perfect union" has been questioned over and over again in the contradictory experiences of people of neglected voices. They live at the edge of our society and cannot afford to embrace our nation's official optimism. The experiences of these people are often invalidated by the majority race people through an unacknowledged "white normativeness," which in fact advances "white privilege." Our prevailing culture of optimism continues to widen the contrasting ways people relate with each other. We see it acknowledged in the terms "Others" and "Othering," which have become common expressions of the dynamic of oppositional relationships prevalent today. As long as aspirational yearning alone addresses the future of peoplehood, we will continue to perpetuate and aggravate the oppositional framework starving our relationships. If we are to recognize "Out of many, we" it will require feeling this in the heart—feeling the painful lives of "Others." In order to meet and know those who are the "Other," the whole people need to grow a heart to feel their suffering, but

44. Cone, *Cross and the Lynching Tree*, 41.

not only their pain, their defiant hope as well. The whole people need to own this suffering and the attending hope against hope as an integral part of all our yearnings for a future worth living. Collectively embracing defiant hope in the midst of suffering is the initial act for overcoming the walls of separation between us.

I have said that our official history of peoplehood is framed within a particular Christian theological notion of redemption. The Christian notion of redemption begs to ask, what does it mean to "have the heart to feel" the tragic outlook of life that has been seen as an inconvenient story when it does not fit the redemptive story of the republic? Using this theological metaphor suggests living in the wilderness and not fitting into "the Society of God's saints." It is in the wilderness that we pursue "What does it mean to have the heart to feel the tragic outlook of life?" I propose that this "wilderness way" will involve liberating "we the people" from remaining imprisoned in freedom, not any "freedom" but the particular freedom we have taken for granted, a freedom to pursue the "officially optimistic" posture of life.

I realize that the statement "becoming free from freedom" comes across as an oxymoron. How can one be freed from freedom? My answer is this: Once the notion of freedom based on the yearning for the redemptive and positivistic future is accepted as sacrosanct, it runs the risk of losing its very nature of being free. To put it differently, once freedom is trusted to be the national and public virtue, especially as it is tied to our growing individualistic understanding of selfhood, it risks turning out be a vice. It fails to recognize the depth of pathos experienced by those who are "Others." "Nobody knows the trouble I've seen. Nobody knows my sorrow." "Nobody knows" is how virtue turns to become vice.

Once again I turn to the words of Reinhold Niebuhr in his book, *The Irony of American History*:

> "If virtue becomes vice through some hidden defect in virtue; if strength becomes weakness because of the vanity to which strength may prompt the mighty man or nation; if security is transmuted into insecurity because too much reliance is placed upon it; if wisdom becomes folly because it does not know its own limits—in all such cases the situation is ironic."[45]

In other words, under the state of hyper-separation and inequality freedom becomes oppressive as an ideal, losing its own strength and

45. Niebuhr, *Irony of American History*, xxiv.

original intent. Freedom becomes an "instrument" of governance, not the original purpose of fostering the respect for individual dignity within the context of the relational life with our neighbors. Freedom takes on the character of being absolute and not the reminder of being a regulator of relationships. Once freedom becomes the "trademark" of the redemptive framework of history, it runs the risk of not considering other frameworks of history, particularly those articulated by the inconvenient voices that talk of the pathos of life. These are the voices that challenge the established framework of freedom within an officially optimistic outlook on the future. These are the voices that reveal the ironic vice we are living today.

THE TENACITY OF ASPIRATIONAL HOPE

The positivistic outlook of a life of freedom is so tenacious in our society. The tenacity lies in the very bond that is upheld publicly to hold people together as the nation, the official striving toward life, liberty, and the pursuit of happiness. It was no accident that the preamble to the US Constitution began with the statement: "We the People of the United States, in Order to form a *more perfect* Union . . ." (emphasis mine). The "more perfect Union" is steeped in a Christian theological view of "a progressive union between the society of God's being and the society of God's saints which is the eschatological goal of creation."[46] This language is full of confidence in the future goal of attaining the "oneness" of *e pluribus unum*, lived out through a more perfect union. Unlike mere wishful thinking, this confidence wells up from the union of mind and heart, a faith in the absolute sovereignty of God in the work through redemptive history.

The establishment of the Constitution embodies this particular theological aspirational version of faith. Justice, tranquility, common defense, promotion of the general welfare, securing "the Blessings of Liberty to ourselves and our Posterity" are what we aspire to and believe in. Our American form of democracy as it is expressed in the Declaration of Independence, the Constitution, and the Bill of Rights, is meant to hold people together, to become "one," through a shared aspirational faith in a particular orientation to an eschatological historical progression. This means the nature of governing our people does not derive solely from executive orders, government programs and regulations, legislative efforts, and judicial decisions. These are means by which the political system functions for the "society of

46. Van Allen, ed., *American Religious Values and the Future of America*, 18.

God's saints." It is no accident that scholars of American history refer to the "soul" of America.

It is generally assumed that the soul of governing rests in an ability of people to bring about the common good as ordained by a divine redemptive process. As long as this theological worldview is taken for granted, even tacitly, then the nation can be intact. But this worldview even as it has evolved into civil religion is increasingly questioned in light of our growing diversity, with a plural reading of what it means to be a people. This is the situation we find ourselves in today as the assumed "oneness" becomes polarized and therefore questionable.

The positivistic framework of peoplehood comes from yet another Christian theological notion, that of what Douglas John Hall calls "sinful presumption." According to Hall, sinful presumption points to the idea of human mastery over nature and history.[47] Sinful presumption is our self-confidence in creating history and directing "nature." This presumption is behind "the doctrine of progress" and "the doctrine of work."[48] Hall's reading is congruent with Niebuhr's assessment that "The dominant note in modern culture is not so much confidence in reason as faith in history."[49] This is a faith in history where the human being is the "master" of his/her fate. However, Hall's mastery narrative does not derive solely from any innate trust in the human ability to meet the challenges of life as it does in the Enlightenment, Age of Reason era. For Hall, the mastery narrative is first of all historically contextual. It derives from a particular time and space in the evolution of Western Enlightenment. It comes out of our particular brand of trust in the "progress" that we have created and then witnessed in history. The mastery narrative is an anticipated new image of human beings, the autonomous determiner of our own destiny.[50] This new image says: "I am the master of my fate; I am the captain of my soul."[51] In American civil religion, this image has taken center stage in a national civil religion, influenced perhaps by French philosopher Jean-Jacques Rousseau and others.

The mastery image, *imago hominis,* emerged "about the same time the New World came into being. *Imago hominis* was indeed responsible for the

47. Hall, *Lighten Our Darkness,* 46.
48. Hall, *Lighten Our Darkness,* 54.
49. Niebuhr, *Faith and History,* 3.
50. Hall, *Lighten Our Darkness,* 45.
51. Hall, *Lighten Our Darkness,* 46.

'discovery' and 'development' of that new world, with man at the center."[52] "The new *imago* was a revolt against the domination of man by divine/demonic powers, and their earthly representatives. Instead of envisaging man under the control of arbitrary, external forces, the new image declared him to be autonomous, the determiner of his own destiny."[53]

This new image of humanity took on a sacred tone in the founding documents of our nation. "We the people" are "ordained" to establish the constitution in order to secure "the Blessings of Liberty to ourselves and our Posterity." In other words, as Reinhold Niebuhr cautions, we the people have forgotten that we are creatures and not the ultimate creators of history. Freedom that originally served as a means to counter the domination of people, particularly domination by the demonic powers of the oppressive institutions of a foreign government, became sacred and regarded as absolute. We the people are here to secure "the Blessings of Liberty to ourselves and our Posterity." We have become the creator and protector of freedom. Freedom has become who we are. In so doing, we have become bound to freedom and constrained by freedom. We have become the prisoner of freedom.

We need to heed the cautionary words of Niebuhr: Mere ignorance is not irony, but ignorance that stems from the pretension of wisdom, self-righteousness, is highly ironic. From a biblical standpoint, the original sin of the garden of Eden, the assumption that we can know everything, continues to plague us. Self-righteousness then becomes the oppositional and contrary way of relating with those who do not share our confidence in our ability to become free and self-determining. Our oppositional ways of relating with people have become harmful as we become hateful of our "enemy," and we fail to the see the irony of our own "innocent" pretensions. In Niebuhr's mind, Abraham Lincoln's performance during the Civil War provides the perfect example of how to remain morally resolute in defense of a free civilization, and yet sufficiently detached so that one can appreciate the incongruities, ironies, and follies of our collective behaviors.

The inconvenient stories of tragedy of the racially minority people and other voices do not fit into the redemptive stories of the American republic because they assault the pretension of wisdom and self-righteousness built into the very foundation of our nation. In other words, the avoidance of tragedy by a majority group leads them to assume that we are not people

52. Hall, *Lighten Our Darkness*, 44.

53. Hall, *Lighten Our Darkness*, 45.

of irony. This willful ignorance is a major cause for the tenacity of national optimism.

However, we should note that the wide acceptance of aspirational optimism in our land cannot be readily dismissed as a racialized narrative of the majority people. Faith in redemptive history is not solely the life outlook of the racial majority people. It has been embraced by minority people as well. Aspirational hope and defiant hope are not an either-or proposition. In our history both can live side by side. Aspirational hope names what peoplehood is about as promised from our beginning. Defiant hope invests in this original promise even while it recognizes the original promise has not been fulfilled. Defiant hope is what drives us to realize the reality of our broken peoplehood that becomes exposed through acknowledging the inconvenient truths of our lived contradictions.

Martin Luther King Jr. said, "Even though we face the difficulties of today and tomorrow, I still have a dream."[54] It is a dream deeply rooted in the American dream, a dream that includes aspirational hope as well as hope against hope. This trust in an aspirational future is shared across race divisions to varying degrees. The "habits of the heart" or, in the words of Jon Meacham, "the soul of America" has a deep resonance for our people everywhere.[55] Parker Palmer says it is deeply ingrained in our "patterns of receiving, interpreting, and responding to experiences that involve our intellects, emotions, self-images, and concepts of meanings and purpose—habits that form the *inward and invisible infrastructure of democracy*."[56]

The aspirational soul of America has guided and sustained both the racial minority and majority people despite the contradictions between our expectations and experiences that continue to plague our peoplehood. The predominantly happy soul, as we have been saying, has great difficulty hearing the experiences of the abyss. Since this is the case, where in our most positive outcome-oriented soul can we find the space to really hear Baldwin's hope against hope words to his nephew: "*The very time I thought I was lost, My dungeon shook and my chains fell off* . . ."? How can we celebrate together the nobility of the human spirit in adversity like those Japanese Americans who went through the concentration camp experiences?

54. King Jr., "I Have a Dream."

55. Palmer, *Healing the Heart of Democracy*, 24.

56. Palmer, *Healing the Heart of Democracy*, 44.

THE REDEEMING OF THE TRAGIC: CRACKING OPEN OFFICIAL OPTIMISM

How do we redeem the inconvenient truths that lurk in the history of the contradictions between expectancy and experience—the truths that refuse to be erased? The words of the preamble of the Constitution, referencing "the Blessings of Liberty to ourselves and our Posterity," have a double meaning, particularly for people of color. These words are a promise that has been broken over and over again. These words give rise to the defiant hope that says the life of pain and suffering will not have the last word. This is a yearning still to be realized. The double message of promise and brokenness tells us that our memories are both lived as well as seen, or in the words of H. Richard Niebuhr, our memories hold both our "internal and external histories." Internal memories are the memories of an event, or series of events that remain in our hearts and continue to impact us deeply. At the same time, the events, if seen from outside, may not leave similar impressions. Niebuhr says:

> Lincoln spoke of what had happened in *our* history, of what had made and formed us and to which we remain committed so long as we continue to exist as Americans; he spoke of purposes which lies in our enduring past and are therefore the purposes of our present life; he described the history of living beings and not data relating to dead things.[57]

What shapes a society is the history that is "lived," not the history "to be seen." Our lives are "caught" by the memories of our heart more than "being taught" by the descriptive lessons we learn about history. Pathos in life does not vanish. It remains both in our personal and corporate lives. Today, the multiple and contrasting heart memories evoked by the promise of "the blessings of liberty" lodged in the preamble is causing a crack in the public optimism of this society that believes it can confidently "form a more perfect union." A vivid diversity stands behind these words revealing where the blessings are given and where blessings are denied, ignored, and covered over. These memories continue to live in our hearts long after the events are forgotten. We see them, we taste them, and we know them in our narratives and in our arts.

The current polarization we are witnessing is not merely the result of people coming together from different backgrounds with each

57. Niebuhr, *Meaning of Revelation*, 45–46.

remembering pathos as well as joy. The critical issue of our day is that people are increasingly fearful and distrustful of the unknown that is present in our differences. And this fear is leading us to see others as opponents and enemies instead of as friends and neighbors. Fear coupled with the aversion to the pathos of those we see as different perpetuates a distrust we have of our neighbors that has become acceptable and normal. Through this aversion to pathos, our relationships have been gradually eroded and broken, making the "blessings of liberty" ring hollow. Our fear and avoidance of our neighbors corrodes the historical habits of the heart that were meant to bring people together.

Tocqueville considered individualism as either a way for a person to willingly work together with others or as an impediment, where individual wants and needs foster a way of isolating us from one another. We call this latter "othering."[58] In other words, individualism can make us think about our own role in the society as a means to bring us together or as something that leads to further fragmentation. Tocqueville scholar Leo Damrosch describes individualism as set within "habits and beliefs [that] are more important than laws are in sustaining liberty."[59] The societal framework of "One out of many," as we are habitually living it at this time, is not capable of bringing people together. Our individualism has become an impediment that has led us into a deepening fragmentation in our society. Our fear of our neighbors resulting from this malignant individualism runs deep, and we must find a way to bridge our differences if we want a future worth living, a future that is not strewn with the fragments of our neighbors' unrealized dreams.

"Othering" has produced exclusion, devaluation, distance, and estrangement in our private and public relationships, rupturing our peoplehood. The result is that we do not know each other nor do we even want to know each other. Frederick Douglass's words about the contradiction in the meaning of the Fourth of July well over a century ago sound tame when we hear Navajo Nation leader Mark Charles speak about the US Constitution as a white supremacist document that does not benefit "Others."[60] The drafting of our Constitution excluded those who were not "We, the People"—the indigenous people, African American slaves, and women of all colors. For some like Charles, the founding documents cannot bring

58. Kaplan, "Political Theory," 14.

59. Damrosch, *Tocqueville's Discovery of America*, 14.

60. Charles, "We the People."

people together today because they are not trustworthy documents for his people. Instead, the Declaration, from his point of view, was a "discovery document" by which the indigenous people were "discovered" and their subhumanness exposed, thus making their presence in North America viewed as dangerous. In other words, the "discovery" of the continent was predicated upon an "uninhabited" land and the nonexistence presence of "human beings." Being "other" than a human being means being treated as invisible and nonsignificant. The Order to "form a more perfect union" turns out to be the opposite of its intended purpose to bring people together. In the meantime, "Others" do not forget that they have not been included in the "discovery" documents. This has led to what we are now experiencing, an increasing disunion of peoplehood, an increasing gap between those who are still not included and those who do not want to know them. All the same, these "Others" remember and live the subhuman categories and treatments deep in their hearts. Our mistrust of each other as a result means we are indeed separate and unequal.

There has been a historically built-in tension between the racially dominant people and the disenfranchised people in understanding the collective narrative of the American people. Within "the spirit of religion and the spirit of liberty," as Alexis de Tocqueville described it, a deep tension has arisen. On the one hand, there is still faith in the aspiring hope for oneness for some, while for others the despair over the lack of oneness continues. For those whose voices have been silenced and excluded from the narrative of hope, a boiling point has been reached. Exclusion has resulted in resentment and distrust on all sides. Those who saw the founding documents created in their absence without their participation find these documents less credible for them.

Jonathan Edwards, a slave owner, preached the importance of submission, not liberation. Historian of race Ibram Kendi says black people have been "stamped from the beginning" as "an ugly stamp on the beautiful," thus seen as inferior to the white population and expected to behave accordingly.[61] "Freedom" was framed as the people from Europe having dominion over the people of color who originated from other continents. Civil rights leader Benjamin Mays's words once again echo this incongruence between liberation for one group and expected submission for another: "I would submit that a nation cannot restore what it has not established. The

61. Kendi, *Stamped from the Beginning*, 3 and 74

nation exempted blacks and, to a large degree, native Americans from the dialectics of freedom. It has not succeeded to this day in including them."[62]

Mays reminded African Americans, and for that matter other people of color, that their life experiences of deep disappointment and their rage over being treated unequally under the officially proclaimed faith in equality, totally undermined the foundation of this nation. The words of the founding documents are now heard to be the words of hypocrisy and deceit for those who were excluded from their formulation. By this route we have reached our disunion! The "soul" of America was not the soul of all people after all. The argument about the democratic principles by which the peoplehood in the US was founded—equality, freedom, and justice—is questioned by large segments of our society. The real "contradiction" of this nation is that the "others" have not really been seen as people. They have not been treated as human beings. As a result, we have begun to hear the alarming voices of these "non-people" in various protest movements of today. These voices are the voices that shout the reality of "separation," "fragmentation," and "polarization."

Unless the voices of previously excluded people are acknowledged, seriously heard, and owned and addressed as "our" voices, the rebirth of peoplehood will not take place. Furthermore, if the participation of the neglected people in the whole makeup of our peoplehood cannot be accomplished, no one will be free. Unless the neglected people are freed, the racially dominant group of people will not be freed from the basic contradiction of this nation! Will new habits of our hearts arise out of this reality of the state of our people today? Patrick Henry's famous words continue to ring in the ears of a large segment of people today: "Is life so dear, or peace so sweet, as to be purchased at the price of chains and slavery? Forbid it, Almighty God! I know not what course others may take, but as for me, give me liberty or give me death!"[63] The words of Frederick Douglass cut through those of Patrick Henry:

> If there is no struggle, there is no progress. Those who profess to favor freedom, and yet depreciate agitation, are men who want crops without plowing up the ground. They want rain without thunder and lightning. They want the ocean without the awful roar of its many waters. This struggle may be a moral one; or it

62. Ahlstrom, in Van Allen, ed., *American Religious Values and the Future of America*, 24.

63. Cited in Wirt, *Life and Character of Patrick Henry*, 119–22.

> may be a physical one; or it may be both moral and physical; but it must be a struggle.[64]

Where do we go from here for a future of peoplehood?

FORGING A NEW FUTURE

"The spirit of liberty" is dangerously divided by extremist actions and untrustworthy political rhetoric. We are currently displaced and dislocated, while "people" are hungry for that which is long-lasting and trustworthy. Where do we go from here? Where do we go to move beyond the despair of uncertainty? Where can we go to get past the fear of the abyss toward the possibility of life, liberty, and the pursuit of happiness? Where do we go from here so that the words of sadness, loss, and rage of the voiceless can be heard and become our own words? Where do we find a forum where our divergent experiences and multiple expectancies can come together? These are the questions facing our peoplehood. Thomas Friedman notes that "our motto used to be 'Out of many, one,' but it's now heading for 'out of many, none.' I fear it could also become 'out of many, me.'" He goes on to say that "I am certain that if we're to thrive in the 21st century it needs to be 'Out of many, we.'"[65] Is "We the People" really possible today in an era of hyper-fragmented life?

Reinhold Niebuhr regarded the essence of faith to be the courage to reflect on the tragic dimension of existence without being "tempted to regard it as meaningless."[66] Perhaps this is the courage we need to face this land of contradictions, the land of separate and unequal. Niebuhr saw the tragedy as the privileged group pitted against the underprivileged in a struggle for righteousness. Our history tells us that the success for such a struggle for justice rests upon the coalition built between the privileged and the underprivileged, a coalition based on the primacy of the relational web of humanity. The relational web is a community of authentic "solidarity" where people hold deep respect for each other. Otherwise, as we have been warned, fierce individualism might eventually isolate Americans one from

64. Douglass, *Frederick Douglass on Slavery and the Civil War*, 42.
65. Friedman, "Let's Change Our Motto to 'Out of Many, We.'"
66. Niebuhr, *Faith and History*, 22.

another, dissolving our commitment to one another, thereby undermining the conditions of freedom for everyone.[67]

Our challenge is to prioritize the web of people within the historically oppositional ways of relating with each other. How can the "human heart of freedom" that pits one against another be persuaded to embrace this web in which we are all entangled? Democracy does not need to function only within a dynamic of opposites. The rebirth of peoplehood needs to question this epistemology of opposites built into *e pluribus unum*, and to explore another epistemology, "out of many, we the web." To engage this "we" way of knowing, the first step is to communicate with each other, so we can learn and know that the fear of our neighbors is our own fear. We need to deeply own that "The life I touch for good or ill will touch another life, and in turn another, until who knows where the trembling stops or in what far place my touch will be felt."[68] And yet under the current climate of polarization, epitomized by what I have called the Ferguson Effect, the very possibility of communication with each other is on life support. The danger we face today is that we have perhaps reached such an extreme pole of hyper-individualism with its oppositional epistemology of relationships that we might not find a way out. But we must. Because the road we are on now ends with the literal death of some individuals, and the demise of whole communities. We have already witnessed to many of these deaths.

A web is not simply the replacement of the historically sacrosanct paradigm of "one" that arises out of many. A replacement of the historically given model is not a realistic answer to the limitations of our familiar paradigm. Our history cannot be reversed. Our history needs to be owned, and its pain needs to be lived, in order to find a new and different way of relating with each other. A relational web can serve as a balm, an alternative aspiration, a true alternative to what we have believed to be the glue that holds us together. Even in a society of rampant individualism "private fulfillment and public involvement are not antithetical."[69] Among those who have bought into radical individualism are those who have also "drawn from an active identification with communities and traditions. . . . Perhaps, as Bellah says, they are so deeply involved with each other that the impoverishment of one entails the impoverishment of the other."[70] Relational people

67. Bellah, "Civil Religion in America," viii.

68. Buechner, *Hungering Dark*, 74.

69. Bellah, "Civil Religion in America," 163.

70. Bellah, "Civil Religion in America," 163.

can arise out of knowing our history of broken relations. They can see and feel the isolation of communities. They can respond to the nagging sense of hollowness in the lofty yet harmful promise of "one." Relational people might entertain alternatives to the futile opposing ways we have been living.

Today we are not merely estranged from our neighbors. We have inherited a condition of estrangement that is decades in the making, and in fact, centuries old. We have become entangled in the distorted ways we have separated ourselves from others through greed and callous self-interests. The tragedy of the contradictions we have inherited is that we find ourselves prevented from consummating our lofty and inspiring ideas of equality, freedom, and justice. We are hobbled by our entanglements in a system that minimizes the experiences of so many. The tragedy is that we lose what we cherish so dearly by devaluing the sufferings and pain of those who are our neighbors, who are really our own siblings. Their lives really are our own lives. The words and ideals that have inspired all people become less credible when we do not honor the actual experiences of all our neighbors. Our peoplehood has this tragic dimension that we must muster the courage to own.

Every account of our life together is shallow if it does not acknowledge tragedy. What can lend us a hand to face this reality? Traditionally, cumulative narratives of faith communities have given us insights into this challenge. The doctrines of sin and love in the Christian faith tradition are examples. But today the fragmented state of many faith communities along with multiple and sometime conflicting interpretations of faith have made it practically impossible for them to provide any credible insights for addressing the tragedy of our broken national peoplehood.

Civil religion, with its positivistic outlook on life, does not seem to help either. As I have been saying, one possible way out of this historical and societal dilemma of tragedy is to listen to the words and stories of those who are strangers, to hear their stories as trustworthy even if they do not coincide with our own experiences. Deep and compassionate listening as exercised in the Truth and Reconciliation Commission of South Africa could provide a model to help us begin a way to courageously face the tragedy we are living. The focus of such listening could be to learn to know about the painful events that happened to people of color, and to investigate the patterns of events that took place over a period of time. But most of all, such a process could at least provide a way for us to meet and engage each other, perhaps meet people we read about in books and newspapers or websites. To hear the voices and see the faces of human beings and their communities most affected by our contradictions might reveal the broken cracks in all of our lives. There is some evidence of this possibility when people and communities let their experiences speak in public.

Will we continue to live with wistful expectancy, or will we face our shared tragedy together? The choice is ours. The challenge is a tall order, but this is precisely the hope against hope for people of color. The hope against hope of mending our torn web just might lead us to tame our shattered and wounded soul of America.

Romney, Garrett, and Putnam say:

> The "we" we were constructing in the first two-thirds of the last century was highly racialized, and thus contained seeds of its own undoing. Any attempt we may make to spark a new upswing must make for a higher summit by being fully inclusive, fully egalitarian, and genuinely accommodating of differences. Anything less will fall victim once again to its own internal inconsistencies.[71]

This is an enormous challenge for the society that has thoroughly embraced an aspirational view of history with its cultivation of radical individualism. Aspirational yearning alone cannot address the future of peoplehood. For we would continue to perpetuate and aggravate the oppositional framework feeding our relationships. Our life together requires feeling the painful lives of "others" and also their defiant hope. Collectively embracing defiant hope is the initial step, and act, of overcoming the walls of separation between us. In the words of Frederick Douglass,

> Banish the idea that one class must rule over another. Recognize the fact that the rights of the humblest citizen are as worthy of protection as are those of the highest, and your problem will be solved; and, whatever may be in store for it in the future, whether prosperity, or adversity; whether it shall have foes without, or foes within, whether there shall be peace, or war; based upon the eternal principles of truth, justice and humanity, and with no class having any cause of complaint or grievance, your Republic will stand and flourish forever.[72]

The challenge is really that of a shared defiant hope. As Meacham said, in order "to create a sphere in which we can live freely, and pursue happiness to the best of our abilities," the shared ownership of defiant hope needs

71. Rosen et al., "Constitution, Elections, and Democracy."

72. Douglass's words quoted by Jamelle Bouie in "Down About the Election?"

to deepen and renew the soul of America.[73] This defiant hope has the "and yet" posture toward the future, where we realize that there is nothing left to lose. Nothing left to lose admits the tragedy of our Broken Heart, so we can begin to mend our self-defeating ways. In the words of Elie Wiesel, "We begin again with night."[74]

The vision of peoplehood—"to sit down together at the table"—is more than ever a necessity. What holds us together as people in the midst of a fractured nation calls for a serious reexamination of the public and hidden assumptions about who we are. No fireworks and patriotic speeches can capture the rebirth of a new peoplehood. Instead, the horse-drawn caisson carrying the body of John Lewis that is deeply etched in our collective memories is the founding "incomparable legacy" of a renewed peoplehood. These new founders beckon us to see the future of our nation through a new lens that sees a relational web of people, not an ideology about national identity, not even the ideology of "oneness" as primary. The future for this new peoplehood is not the unity in diversity of "one out of many." Rather, it is a new way of relating with each other out of our different experiences and diverse groups of people. It means to know that the lives of our neighbors are very much our own. This future will not ignore the long history of the sufferings of racism. It will be a future where we can relate with each other in non-oppositional, non-fragmented, and non-adversarial ways, in equal and just ways. Out of many, a web, may offer a new vision for all people where the well-being of all people will not come at the expense of others. This new vision is planted in and supported by a "hope against hope" shared and practiced by all of us.

73. Meacham, *Soul of America*, 8.

74. Quoted in Reichek, "Elie Wiesel."

CHAPTER FIVE

The Illusion of Precision

I PROPOSE THAT THE problem of the twenty-first century is the problem of treating our neighbors as fearful strangers, not as neighbors upon whom we depend. The historical color lines continue to exist today. But today the color lines make our neighbors mutually fearful even as they continue to help us identify who we are in the society. We are tempted to stay away from our neighbors who are strangers. But strangers do not stay outside of our gates. They have a way of intruding into our lives. Unhoused people are not merely an embarrassment. Their tents are increasingly close to our comfortable homes, reminding us of the disparity and inequality of our life together. We watch the news about our neighbors killing people at school and at malls. All of a sudden we get assaulted out of nowhere. We find ourselves living side by side with our neighbors, but often in fear. This fear is particularly acute for people of color. We are not invisible and confined to the news reporting. We are all around.

More than ever before we find ourselves treating neighbors as potential enemies. The race lines place a stamp of approval to this way of relating with each other. To be sure, some of us do reach out to strangers. Civic organizations and numerous social and faith groups try to treat our neighbors caringly. But the truth is that the hostile and oppositional ways we treat and relate with each other persist and are becoming more prevalent. This is happening even when color lines try to protect people of color from assaults. Black Lives Matter is an example today. The Native American tribes' self-determination movement is another. This is the current landscape of our peoplehood. Color lines exacerbate contradictions and oppositional relationships at the same time they seek to protect and affirm people's identities. However, ever so faintly this historical view of our identities and relationships is shifting. In the midst of rigid views of identities and the resulting brokenness of relationships something new is arising. In the midst of deeply divided views of who we are and how we relate, the question of why Americans are so kind yet so cruel becomes increasingly relevant. It raises new questions about how we understand race today. We are becoming aware that race is much more complex and less clearly definable. Through an historical understanding of ourselves as a peoplehood of contradictions we are gradually beginning to glimpse our "illusion of precision." At the same time, this glimpse is still faint and extremely tentative.

The illusion of precision points to something new, a nomadic way of seeing who we are and the way we relate with each other. It is contrary to any rigid and precise way of seeing our differences. As we begin to see how dependent we are on each other, personally as well as publicly, perhaps we can also begin to approach each other with some kind of genuine longing to know each other. The dawning of this realization comes from recognizing how we really are interdependent, and the possibility that we really do have something in common that we haven't fully acknowledged. This emerging awareness is based on our tentative faith in each other, trusting in the web that holds all of us even in the midst of our brokenness from the oppositional way we have seen differences in the past.

RACIAL HYBRIDIZATION: NEW WAYS OF UNDERSTANDING RACE

The conversation about race has long been that of categorizations, "color lines." This is particularly evident in the societal perceptions of race. For so long race has been seen as a way to categorize people, either for separation or identity-building. Until now race has been regarded as static, stable, with separate categories where a person's biological make-up shapes their identity. "Myths about physical racial differences were used to justify slavery and are still believed by doctors today," says columnist Jamelle Bouie.[1] Categorization of race was used to assume "an undemocratic assumption present at its founding: that some people are inherently entitled to more power than others."[2] At the same time, color lines have also protected people of color. Our histories, how we express ourselves, and the values and ways of living

1. Bouie, "America Holds onto an Undemocratic Assumption," 56.
2. Bouie, "America Holds onto an Undemocratic Assumption," 50.

are our own, not the ways we are perceived by others. Black lives matter indeed! People of color are not honorary whites!

As noted in the previous chapter, people of color bristle when a person of the majority race says to us: "We have always treated you as one of our own." What we hear in what appears to be an innocuous statement is: "As long as you behave in the way we are comfortable with and accustomed to, then we accept you. Once you surprise us with something unconventional and foreign to us, we become suspicious of you. We are not sure if you can be trusted." The hidden message is: "You appear to us a perpetual foreigner and you do not belong here." Race categorization can work to protect people of color from such assumed expectations that commodify us and erase our worth and dignity. Race categories have long been treated as both affirmative of our dignity and as an assault to our beings.

However, today race also has to do with the various roles a person or a group of people plays in society as well as the evolving perceptions of race that the person or group provides. The role race plays in our changing perceptions often changes and evolves. It is not always stable. Correspondingly, the changing roles and perceptions also shift the meaning of the relationships we have professionally, societally, and personally. The limitations of race classifications are revealing the growing awareness that race is an "illusion of precision". The categorizing of race that has been our accustomed way of approaching racial difference is beginning to shift.

The 2020 National Census indicates an increase of 276 percent in those who claim two or more racial identifications, making up what is known as the multiracial population. Whereas those who identify only as white declined by 8.6 percent since 2010.[3] "These changes reveal that the U.S. population is much more multiracial and more diverse than what we measured in the past."[4] This is the landscape of the American peoplehood today.

The historical categorization of race is changing today. For African Americans, the "one drop rule" legally codified and categorized individuals of African heritage as singularly black, justifying enslavement and segregation. It led to the default racial power structure in the US as a black and white dyad. To a large measure, this dyad perception is still assumed in the United States when race is analyzed. This means that other people of color and multiracial people are often left out and made invisible. Their

3. USAFACTS.org, "Our Changing Population."

4. USAFACTS.org, "Our Changing Population."

existence has often been overlooked or even erased in our history, as in the case of Native Americans. The increasing number of multiracial people is particularly overlooked because multiracial people do not conform to the monoracial static categorizing of race. Given this historical neglect there have been a growing number of voices and alternative theories of race that challenge this dyadic paradigm.

The increasing number of those who consider themselves multiracial and hybridized experience themselves ever more as invisible in our society. These are people who defy the conventional categorizations of race. To more intentionally seek them out and hear their stories would create a different and valuable way to understand the meanings of race and racial identities today. We need to ask about the role this emerging segment can play in the future of peoplehood.

What needs to be emphasized about multiracial people is that our experiences and identities are very diverse and cannot be readily classified in the conventional and official ways racial groups have been classified. Such designations as American Indian, black, Asian, Latino, Native Hawaiian, white and some others, as they are listed in the US census, no longer fit.[5] While boundary-based notions of race still speak to a large number of people of color, many multiracial people do not see themselves in this way. Furthermore, there is a temptation to consider people's diverse and unconventional identity expressions, particularly those of multiracial people, as a reason to dismiss their voices in the conversations about race today. This tendency to dismiss multiracial voices points to our need to pay particular attention to our illusions of precision about race today.

There are both historical and future-shaping factors that need to be brought into the conversation about the role multiracial and hybridized people play in the evolving subject of peoplehood. Historically, a strong racial and ethnic identity contributed to both the development of personal identity and a sense of well-being for people of color. It also helped defend against their devaluation by the racially dominant group. Self-worth and confidence can derive from the positive racial image of oneself and one's community, particularly in the world where race has equaled rejection, invisibility, and devaluation, and being seen as "less than" the dominant race. There are rich and deep cultures that have shaped our identities. At the same time, there is the paradox of identity formation as a person also becomes aware of their identity being negatively formed. In some, this has

5. U.S. Decennial Census Measurement of Race and Ethnicity.

led to the development of an "internalized racism," where negative racial stereotype got embedded in their identity formation. Developing a strong racial-ethnic identity is at once a critical protective factor and a diminishment of self-worth for people of color.

An added factor for multiracial people is that they have multiple identities as well as the freedom not to be bound by the familiar boundary-based notion of race. Multiracial persons might choose to identity as a member of one of their monoracial groups. Or, they may claim to be multiracial, biracial, mixed race, or some newly invented term to encompass their self-perception. They may also change and create an identity depending on their relationships to different contexts and situations. Some may even refuse to identify racially! There really is no predictable pattern of racial identification for this group of people. At the same time, the historical categorization of race stubbornly persists in our society, even with the increasing hybridization of people. What can confidently be foreseen is that the multiracial population will continue to increase in our society and the racial landscape of our peoplehood will be impacted by their numbers. What impact this increase will have remains to be seen.

RACIAL FORMATION AFFECTS US ALL

Sociologists Michael Omi and Howard Winant have proposed "racial formation" as a way of treating and understanding race in this fast-changing society. Instead of treating race as some kind of static identity, Omi and Winant treat race as a matter of contextual formation. They emphasize social structures and sociocultural representations with individual meaning as well as collective actions that take place within the historical change.[6] Given the plethora of factors such as the civil rights movement, the war on terror, and gender debates, the current polarizations impact the meaning of race. The question becomes more and more complex and in need of nuance in our shifting landscape of peoplehood. Omi and Winant respond to this question with the notion of racial formation:

> [R]acial formation is the sociohistorical process by which racial categories are created, reified, challenged, and transformed. It is the shifting construction of racial meanings formed in the

6. Omi and Winant, *Racial Formation in the United States: From the 1960s to the 1990s.* (This book has gone through three editions since its first publication in 1986. The quotations in this work are from the edition listed here.)

> dialectic between state categorization and social challenges to those categorizations, and the sociohistorical process by which racial meanings are created, lived, and transformed . . .
>
> The racial order is equilibrated by the state, encoded in law, organized through policy-making, and enforced by a repressive apparatus. But the equilibrium thus achieved is unstable, for the great variety of conflicting interests encapsulated in racial meanings and identities cannot be more than pacified at best by the state.[7]

In this densely packed statement is the reality of race in the US. Racial categories are determined by social, economic, and political forces. Thus, peoplehood cannot be understood without acknowledging race and its various meanings that pervade our society, from the shaping of individual identities to the very structure of collective political actions of our society. The racial landscape is shifting, and race issues are becoming more pronounced in the eye of the public. We begin to see more clearly how poverty is racialized. Race has become recognized as a major factor in healthcare in light of the COVID-19 pandemic. Race has been brought back into the foreground through Black Lives Matter, with its attention to race in the criminal justice system. The exposure of "Invisible Asian Americans" syndrome in the current violence against them is another example. A profound shift is taking place in race matters, a shift that Omi and Winant name as a "disruption of preconceived notions of race expectations," where "the unending faux pas committed by whites who assume that the non-whites they encounter are servants or tradespeople, the belief that non-white are less qualified persons to fulfill affirmative action guidelines . . ."[8] These negative tropes are being called out. Racial formation theory describes racial categorization developmentally.

Race, as it is currently categorized, is cast as legitimate and normative, which then becomes a "normal" part of society with the result that the dominant groups gain control over the disenfranchised people. Powers and principalities of racial injustices take on this creeping and insidious character. Officially sanctioned racism through its codified policies becomes accepted as normal and legitimate by dominant groups. Injustices get enacted according to whatever the purpose these taken-for-granted racial categories serve to maintain the dominance over the racially disadvantaged

7. Omi and Winant, *Racial Formation in the United States*, 53–59.

8. Omi and Winant, *Racial Formation in the United States*, 59.

groups. When these "preconceived notions of a racialized social structure" are disrupted, the disruption produces profound effects in the way race is apprehended and its discussion publicly played out.[9]

THE ILLUSION OF PRECISION

Racially motivated societal projects "mediate between discursive or representational means in which race is identified and signified on the one hand, and the institutional and organizational forms in which is it routinized and standardized on the other."[10] Race discourse is caught between these mediating factors. The dynamic and fluid landscape of race amidst the "preconceived notion" of race classifications is not merely a new phenomenon. Significantly, the impact of the shifting race landscape with its accompanying "disruption of expectations" could be profound. This dynamic and shifting racial landscapes can be characterized as an "illusion of precision."[11] The term comes from architectural philosopher Jorge Arango.

> This is when something looks so polished that it leads you to believe it's been thought through, when it actually hasn't. It's not a final proposal, only a first stab at the form that will address the content. Unfortunately, the way it is communicated leads people to misinterpret it as a more stable than it actually is. . . . First drafts will be rough, but they must still convey meaning. The right level of fidelity will depend on what the thing being designed is and the needs of the terms involved. As a design leader, it's important that you set expectations clearly, so people don't assume they're looking at something more polished than it's supposed to be.[12]

The illusion of precision describes the current status of race and introduces new challenges that have not been considered in previous understandings of race. Race, understood as borders and barriers that enclose people within the safety of familiar territories, can also become a confined space beyond reason or necessity. As mentioned earlier, race can provide both separation and solidarity amongst people. It is tempting to cling to this more static understanding of race in our currently unsettled, unpredictable, unstable, and changing environment of race. Perhaps we still long for the precision of

9. Omi and Winant, *Racial Formation in the United States*, 60.
10. Omi and Winant, *Racial Formation in the United States*, 60.
11. "The illusion of precision" was also employed in my *The Color of Faith*.
12. Arango, "Meaning in Translation."

a label. We prefer clarity and familiarity and want to distance ourselves from the unknown, unfamiliar, and unexpected. But we will be hampered by this familiar way of understanding ourselves if we do not become open to our changing race landscape. The recent National Census reveals that over 27 percent of American people identify with two or more racial populations. Moreover, those who identify as white declined by nearly 9 percent since 2010. "The U.S. population is much more multiracial and more diverse than what we measured in the past."[13]

Once our own lives become unstable and move away from the familiar life of the past, a new truth begins to emerge. Those who have been seen as the dominant group of people tend to continue to live the illusion of precision. Their understandings of race remain stable and unchanged. For those who inhabit the "underside" of life, however, our multiracial neighbors become strangely "familiar" and knowable. Moreover, those who are at the "upper side" of the currently segregated society, a fixed understanding of race can become a safe means for associating with those from whom they are segregated. This happens because of the way peoplehood has functioned almost by necessity. We are relational beings. Those who live on the "upper side" of peoplehood end up relating with those on the "underside" one way or another. We can segregate and separate them, but their existence still impacts us. We live a "functional" familiarity based on an illusion of precision, with its attending "kind" behaviors toward unfamiliar neighbors as well as unspoken "cruel" gestures to these same strangers.

How did racial categorizing come about? It started with the slavery of Africans when segregation was imposed on relationships between neighbors. Its consequences continue today because the manner in which we relate with our neighbors has remained relatively unchanged. The categorizing pattern continues in respect to other racialized groups. The isolation of Japanese Americans into concentration camps during World War II is an example of this. And it did not end with the conclusion of the war. It has surfaced again in the recent "violence against Asian Americans." We see it again affecting the lives of the recent undocumented people who enter the US. The incidents of segregation and its consequences are quite alive today.

Segregation, isolation, and the erasure of painful memories of events do not work. It is an illusion to think we can "define" those with whom we relate. It is an illusion to think we can define our spaces where we live as places apart from those we think of as other. They have a way of reentering

13. USAFACTS.org, "What Does the Census Mean by 'Some Other Race'?"

our lives to haunt us. We see this in the growing number of unhoused people who are all around in our cities. They become "familiar" to us as they crowd our walkways and sleep in our doorways. Sick people impose themselves. Lonely people seek us out. In addition, there are angry people who cause gun violence, and by it they are no longer invisible strangers. These so-called strangers live among us. They could well be our next-door neighbors. The pain of strangers is no longer only their pain. It belongs to everyone, even if the powerful and comfortable try to avoid it. This is the true meaning of what philosopher Theodor Adorno means when he talks about exile as "not being at home in one's own home."[14] The exilic life means to remain safely imprisoned in the illusionary life of exclusion and isolation with prejudice against those we perceive to be different and inferior. In this lifestyle we deceive ourselves and diminish our own well-being. What I am suggesting is that an alternative to this exile is the nomadic life of "not being at home in our own home." The nomadic life is one where all illusions of precisions fade away.

The illusion of precision captures the future of our racial landscape and its significance for our society in at least two ways. First, racial categorization is becoming less precise in the midst of the rampant racism that still persists. There are increasing numbers of those who see themselves as "disoriented selves" who do not fit into the existing racial classifications.[15] Racial identities are at once stronger than ever for many communities such as Black Lives Matter, while the meaning of identity become less precise and shifting for others. Contradictions of racial identities are becoming more pronounced. But literature scholar Lisa Lowe cautions that hybridization of race "is not the 'free' oscillation between or among chosen identities." She observes that hybridization, the illusion of precision of race, "is an uneven process through which immigrant communities encounter the violences of the U.S. state."[16] In other words, multiracial and hybridized people continue to encounter persistent racism in their imprecise racial categories. Owning an illusion of precision does not directly eliminate all forms of racism. In a multiracial view of race, the previous meanings of racial identity are not so polished and are still in a "rough draft" phase of understanding. Entering

14. Adorno quoted by Said, *Exile*, 184.

15. This is the term used for non-monoracial people by Rudy Busto, University of California Santa Barbara.

16. Lowe, *Immigrant Acts*, 82.

a nomadic and disorienting way of life's meanings deeply challenges the stability of life.

An illusion of precision in race points beyond the fluidity of the boundary-setting categorization of racial identities to how we live a quality level of life. The illusion of precision forces us to engage matters of value, orientations, and outlooks on life. It is a shift from a stable meaning of life to an awareness of an unsettled state of life experiences and our sense of identities that no longer fit conventional wisdom. Postcolonial scholar Edward Said talks about the meaning of exile as a state of terminal loss. He says that "the achievements of exile are permanently undermined by the by the loss of something left behind forever."[17] As Adorno says, the exilic life points to the "morality of not being at home in one's own home."[18] The illusion of precision of race ends similarly in the state of being nomadic, that is the state of terminal loss of the "precisely" crafted rigid notion of life.

How will the phenomenon of "not being at home in one's own home" impact the future of peoplehood? Here Said is helpful. He relates terminal loss with the cultural impact exile has had on the modern West. He says: "modern Western culture is in large part the work of exiles."[19] And, "our age . . . is indeed the age of the refugee, the displaced." What people in exile strive for is "to create a new world that is "unnatural and its unreality resembles fiction."[20] Disorientation affects everyone, both those who consider their identities stable for one reason or another, and those who undergo the nomadic life. Remember, when a thread of the web of our peoplehood is touched, it sets the whole web trembling. When the illusion of precision about race is exposed, when we know we are in a changing and nomadic state of peoplehood, when the state of terminal loss of precise racial classifications takes hold, then the familiar world gives way to a new world that is unnatural, and its unreality resembles fiction. The significance of this aspect of the illusion of precision that is taking place in racial dynamics needs further exploration, especially as we continue to explore the changing meaning of "diversity."

17. Said, *Exile,* 173.

18. Adorno quoted by Said in *Exile,* 184.

19. Said, *Exile,* 173.

20. Said, *Exile,* 181.

E PLURIBUS UNUM RECONSIDERED

The subject of the illusion of precision helps deepen and focus the meaning of a nation of contradictions. What will it mean to live with differences, especially the differences that deeply alienate one person and group from another? What will it mean to do this at the same time we continue to consent to journey together even with our differences? The illusion of precision is now placed within the question of how to advance the conversation of the future of a peoplehood burdened with historically embedded contradictions. How does the illusion of precision aid or hinder promoting "the general Welfare, and secur[ing] the Blessings of Liberty to ourselves and our Posterity"? This question resides in the epistemological realm. How might relinquishing our illusion of precision help us live together as the polarized people who have long been related to each other in opposition? When our own identities and ways of relating with each other are more fluid and nomadic, how will this affect the ways that we relate? This change of epistemological framework is already operating in gender studies in recent years. Nonbinary identities are more prevalent today. Perhaps they will help guide us forward.

An age of instability and nomadic unpredictability will involve a change of paradigms, a shift of understanding peoplehood as "oneness" to people on a "journey" we take together. This is perhaps the most daunting challenge facing the future of peoplehood in the United States. Racism, whether it is viewed systemically or personally, will be seen differently. The illusion of precision comes from questioning the perception of what is "natural" and "real" for us. "Natural" and "real" all these years and centuries have become the accepted and more or less precise values and norms for measuring one another on the basis of the way we look, and the color of our skin. Racism, in other words, has been a way of seeing and relating with people based on what "appears" to the majority race population. As noted, this has provided a false justification for the fear and distrust as a basis for our relationships.

Racism is a highly subjective and arbitrary perception of people by those who have been conditioned by the norms and values that have been historically established in gauging people. When the illusion of precision is accounted for, when differences are not so pronounced, when we become aware of "not being at home in our own home," then what brings people together is no longer the presumed commonality of people. People cannot be brought together out of the old "One from many" when it is reinterpreted through a lens of fluid identities. We know that has hurt people of color.

The illusion of precision is a complicated reality for people who assert their separate and unique selves while living a self in a relational climate that is not so precise. Deep care and wisdom will be needed to dispel our illusions of precision while keeping our necessary differences intact. How will the illusion of precision intersect with the need to still claim distinctness? In this regard, the authentic goal of true mutuality cannot be abandoned or short-circuited. In one respect, recognizing the complicated interplay between the illusion of precision and our distinct place in relationships confirms just how interrelated we are in our web of life together.

What does *e pluribus unum* mean in a world full of "disoriented" people with shifting identities? Historically the *unum*, "oneness," has been understood as "likeness" and "resemblance," that is the presence of similarity or commonality in spite of differences. These assumptions speak to the weight of the challenge facing the rebirth of peoplehood. *Unum* is not a value-neutral word. *Unum* suggests a facsimile, a copy, to whatever is original. "Oneness" is not an original. The history of our peoplehood was originally "uncommon." This is the real foundation upon which our so-called "oneness" has been constructed. What was uncritically considered to be "common" was never mutually owned and agreed upon. Commonality is shaped on the basis of a history arbitrarily fashioned and laden with particular noncompatible values and power dynamics. In the meantime, as Said reminds us, we have constructed barriers to try to hide this truth: "Borders and barriers, which enclose us within the safety of familiar territory, can also become prison and are often defended beyond reason or necessity."[21] We desperately need a different model, a new foundation, shaped by "non-master's tools," that acknowledges the parity of each participant who comes together for a shared future worth living. Simply put, *e pluribus unum* needs to be placed in a new illusion-free framework of separate and equal.

The shift of *e pluribus unum,* "out of many, one" to "out of many, a web" might give rise to a people on a journey together. It could even create a new story of people living together, not based on an abstract ideal no matter how noble the ideal may be, but on a shared, living journey where real conflicts and contradictions are not hidden, but embraced, for the sake of everyone. Such a shift cannot be accomplished merely at the level of spiritual metanoia on the part of individuals or even interpersonal endeavors.

21. Said, *Exile,* 185.

Such a shift will require a major disruption of power dynamics operating at the basic structure of our society. It will require the admission of the brokenheartedness of our history that infects our communal life today. The disruption that will be required will not occur as long as the normativeness of human worth and values are fixed and unbending, lodged in familiar and stable notions of life.

If the current demographic trends continue toward the disruption of our illusion of the precision, a basic shift in the way we relate with each other may already be in the making. If multiracial identities continue to challenge the entrenched perception-based valuation and classification of race, and if the unstable nomadic life of hybridized people gradually dominates race relations, then there may be opportunities for new and "unnatural" imaginations to be seen and heard. These new imaginings hold a promise for new ways to relate with each other, without the opposing and hostile postures toward those who appear "different." But this cannot be seen as an easy, or even an expected transition. The cost of claiming a multiracial or nonbinary racial identity is high, because to do so places oneself and the community where one belongs in the position of becoming even more marginalized in a society unwilling to change. In other words, one becomes vulnerable to exile. "Exile means that you are always going to be marginal, and that what you do . . . has to be made up because you cannot follow a prescribed path."[22] This exilic posture of life is totally contrary to the American dream of "happiness" in the popular understanding of that term, or any claim to "exceptionalism," if that means superior to others in terms of moral and just character. To reconsider *e pluribus unum* today means to wake up to the brokenhearted legacy of this motto and attend to the need for deep healing in our communities and nation. In other words, to reconsider *e pluribus unum* today means waking the dead! Waking the sleepwalkers whose eyes are closed to their neighbors, and therefore to themselves as well!

Gary Dorrien quotes Walter Earl Fluker to comment on the shifting role of black churches today. "The calling of church leaders in King's time was to stir the churches to struggle for freedom and equality. The calling of church leaders today is to wake the dead."[23] By this, Fluker calls for black Americans to move from exodus to exile, to diaspora from liberation. "Those who are driven to the wilderness do not seek to make straight that

22. Said, *Exile*, 181.

23. Dorrien, "Walter Earl Fluker's Call to Black Church," 26.

which is crooked. They do not assume responsibility for the right ordering of the world. They dare to speak for themselves, the voices of the muted, missed, and dismissed, the wretchedly fated who have no recourse but to cry out."[24]

"There is a silence that I cannot speak. There is a silence that will not speak," says Japanese Canadian writer Joy Kogawa.[25] The underlying values of peoplehood encompass both voice and silence, even a forced silence. This is what it means to be marginal. `This is what it means to be an exile. Yet, the way out of exile is to embrace a nomadic life thrust upon us by relinquishing our illusions of precision. This nomadic spirituality is a way of saying that we live in an alienated state one from another, that we are indeed islands all along. But we are not called to stay there permanently. To admit we are exiled islands is a necessary precondition for genuine trust and desire to arise in order to reach out to another person. Counterintuitively, to become aware that we are actually "an island" can lead us to embrace a new reality where "No one is an island." We are simply nomads on an uncertain journey together!

A nomadic life orientation undergoes constant negotiations between the antipathy of racism and a longing for liberating relationship between people. As Lowe points out, the hybridization of race is an "uneven process." Those who embrace it survive the violence they encounter while "living, inventing, and reproducing different cultural alternatives."[26] What we are experiencing today, hyper-differentiation and hyperpolarization, reveals to us that when you strike any part of the web, you start the whole web trembling. The oppositional ways we relate with each other have imposed a cost. The cost is we live in the midst of heartbreak whether we acknowledge it or not. That was what John Lewis did. He lived in the midst of pain both of others and his own. He then called people together. He rallied communities, even those who were discouraged, to summon a better future, and to mend the tattered web of peoplehood. He did this not just for Americans of African descent, but for all people. To live a nomadic life means to acknowledge our inability to draw a blueprint for the future, but to confess our complicity in perpetuating the adversarial ways we relate with each another—and the ways we continue to neglect those who live at the edge of the society. To say that the nomadic life is a viable way forward is to hope

24. Dorrien, "Walter Earl Fluker's Call to Black Church."

25. Kogawa, *Obasan*, 14.

26. Lowe, *Immigrant Acts*, 82.

against hope. Yet, such hope is worth living. As Leonard Cohen explains about his song "Hallelujah," "This world is full of conflicts and full of things that cannot be reconciled. But there are moments when we can reconcile and embrace the whole mess, and that's what I mean by 'Hallelujah.'"[27] In other words, we really do not know what we don't know. Imprecision is the way forward. That is a glimpse of the future of peoplehood in this land.

27. Fetters, "How Leonard Cohen's 'Hallelujah' Became Everybody's 'Hallelujah.'"

CONCLUSION

Joining Trusted Stories

HISTORY THAT SPEAKS TO OUR HEART

THIS CONCLUDING CHAPTER COULD serve as the introduction to this work. But I decided to locate this chapter at the end of the whole work. The reason is that I would like to let the whole narration of my confessional reading of peoplehood unfold on its own without the conclusion carrying the weight of the whole work. The subject of this book is the redemption of the soul of American peoplehood from the perspective of race relations. I approached this subject from my own personal experience of American history. "Confession" is my *modus operandi* for this work. The meaning of peoplehood is understood differently and divergently depending on the time and place of the interpreters. So, I am aware that my reading is not a final word on this subject. Therefore, my method of approaching this highly complex and broad subject is confessional and not propositional in nature. What do I mean by approaching American peoplehood "confessionally"? I mean by this term my own reading of the unfolding of our history through a particular lens. As noted earlier, theologian H. Richard Niebuhr in *The Meaning of Revelation* talks about the difference between "history as seen" and "history as lived." Approaching history confessionally means for me approaching "history as lived." This way of engaging history is viewed "not (as) the succession of events which an uninterested spectator can use from the outside but our own history."[1] History as lived is treated as that which speaks to our hearts, individual and communal hearts, not merely to our

1. Niebuhr, *Meaning of Revelation*, 44.

heads. Moreover, history as lived functions to "illuminate" what might otherwise be dismissed as a random series of events we experience in life. For Niebuhr history as lived is "revelation."

> When we speak of revelation, we mean that something has happened to us in our history which conditions all our thinking and that through this happening we are enabled to apprehend what we are, what we are suffering and doing and what our potentialities are.[2]

For our discussion of American peoplehood, when we talk about the bond that holds us together, as Niebuhr says, "we mean that special occasion which provide[s] us with an image by means of which all the occasions of personal and common life become intelligible."[3] The "One" as noted in the founding documents, is a case in point. The "one" of our "seen" history as reported by "an uninterested spectator" is conventionally understood as the sameness that lives in separateness. But it can be also viewed as a "lived" history of the heart where people "journey together" even though we live in a torn web of relationships. These images are powerful symbols by which our own lives could become intelligible if our history is viewed by all of us "internally."

We have said our peoplehood is one of contradictions. Out of this realization, my confession is that we are a people of the broken heart. If we realize the brokenness of our communal heart, then we might move toward a gentler and kinder way of treating each other instead of perpetuating competitiveness and cruelty. The question is, can these realizations speak to our hearts deeply? Can the "realization" of our brokenhearted way of life be an authentic and motivating revelation?

"Revelation" in our case is not the specific event of Christ that Niebuhr's book addresses. Rather, the "revelation" that is explored in this work is an admission of the history of contradiction—the presence of kindness and cruelty in our history as the foundation of our life together. Revelation in this book makes visible the brokenhearted people who know from experience that a natural unfolding or progress toward unity that overcomes whatever challenges that come our way, is a false promise. I am aware that my perspective is limited. My intention for approaching this question is to advance a public and ongoing conversation, not to invite the readers to agree or disagree with my reading of this difficult and controversial subject.

2. Niebuhr, *Meaning of Revelation*, 100.

3. Niebuhr, *Meaning of Revelation*, 80.

I am inviting readers into a reexamination of the assumptions we bring to the question of what holds people together. I am hoping readers will revisit our history, and possibly explore ways we can modify our behaviors toward each other. This is the methodological framework of the "lived," confessional history I bring to this work.

BECOMING AND BELONGING INTO PEOPLEHOOD BY "CONSENT"

> We hold these truths to be self-evident, that all men are created equal, that they are endowed by their Creator with certain unalienable Rights, that among these are Life, Liberty and the pursuit of Happiness. —That to secure these rights, Governments are instituted among Men, deriving their just powers from the consent of the governed.

We yearn for the words of our founders to become truly our own consented words. For true consent we need to travel a journey of owning the contradictory truths of who we have been, who we are, and who we want to become. We will have to face how the dissonance of being both kind and cruel on the part of too many has impacted the people who have been most affected and not heard. The word "consent" as the tool for democracy is both the act of owning the historical reality of our brokenness and the quest of establishing true equality in the midst of this tragic reality.

"Consent" is a collective endeavor, a willingness to live with those who we do not know well, including those with whom we do not see eye to eye. Agreement is a contract. "Consent" involves relationship building. I would maintain that "consent" as described here and as stated in our founding document is the true meaning of *E Pluribus unum.* It is a lingering hunger to mend our broken relationship even though we have been unable to do so, as demonstrated in our history. I believe, I hope against hope, that the slender thread of hunger that pulls us toward mending our relationships will be able to reweave our communities. This hunger just might stir us to an authentic *unum* because of a new "consent" to our brokenness. But this is still our deepest challenge. As noted earlier, while defiant hope has survived all this time, there is no guarantee it will always continue. How long can this hope remain unfulfilled? This is a central question facing race relations today. Sadly, we continue to relate with each other in oppositional ways. This is the character of the people of contradictions. We continue to deeply cherish our "individual" freedom as we live together with our neighbors we hardly know. "Consent" is the word chosen by the founders to narrate this contradiction. If the original choice of the word "consent" reveals even a hint of our hunger for authentic relationship, perhaps this word can still be trusted,

We have not been good at welcoming and complementing strangers. "Complemental" relationships belong to a "thin tradition," to use the term of theologian Douglas John Hall. A thin tradition lurks within a dominant set of traditions. America's "optimistic" outlook on life is part of the dominant traditions, along with oppositional ways of relating. The thin tradition in American practices of relating can be called complementary because it emerges in the midst of "a broken statement about life's brokenness." As Hall says, the thin tradition participates in what it seeks to describe.[4] Reformer Martin Luther was another theologian who recognized the role of the thin tradition when he described the person as one who witnesses to it "by living, by dying and being damned, not by understanding, reading and speculating."[5] It is difficult for the members of the white dominant culture to appreciate our "thin tradition" engendered by brokenness. Because, in the words of James Cone, "Whites today cannot separate themselves from the culture that lynched blacks, unless they confront their history and expose the sin of white supremacy."[6] In other words, the dominant culture is satisfied with "seen history" as authentic history. This is the reality of the broken web of humanity as we probe the rebirth of peoplehood.

The glue that brings people together is not an agreement of ideas, no matter how noble the ideas are. Instead, the basic glue of peoplehood is the web that is viewed from the vantage point of a relational framework, a "non-master's" framework. The basic glue has to do with becoming good neighbors to each other, and this is the matter of "consent." bell hooks was aware of this when she wrote the oft-quoted words, "I am often struck by the dangerous narcissism fostered by spiritual rhetoric that pays so much attention to individual self-improvement and so little to the practice of love within the context of community."[7]

4. Hall, *Lighten Our Darkness*, 117.

5. Quoted by Rupp, *Righteousness of God*, 227.

6. Cone, *Cross and the Lynching Tree*, 165.

7. hooks, *All About Love*, 76.

CONSENT WITHIN THE OPPOSITIONAL WAY OF RELATIONSHIPS

Democracy, particularly the representative democracy that we have sought to uphold in our land, is the way we understand and regulate our behaviors. Democracy, according to the original founding documents, is possible only for those who possess the "unalienable rights" to "consent," that is, collectively "strive" for the understandings and regulations that make democracy possible. We collectively strive "to secure these rights, governments are instituted among men [*sic*], deriving their just power from the consent of the governed," says the Constitution. According to the founders the attainment of these rights that bring people together rests in a government whose power and authority rests in the democratic "consent of the governed"—the consent of the organized people. What underlies the "consent" then is what Alexis de Tocqueville calls the "habits of the heart," deeply ingrained into a "people's" way of being, seeing, and reacting to life that wells up from their hearts, not just from their heads. "The human heart is the first home of democracy," says educator Terry Tempest Williams. She asks a series of questions: "Can we be equitable? Can we be generous? Can we listen with our whole beings, not just our minds, and offer our attention rather than our opinions?"[8] The answers to these questions underscore what it takes to consent.

The "inalienable rights" as an aspirational promise for equality in the midst of separateness gets codified into laws and regulations through the "consent" of those whose "hearts" are collectively represented. Educator Parker Palmer describes the "habits of the heart" as "deeply ingrained patterns of receiving, interpreting, and responding to experiences that involve our intellects, emotions, self-images, and concepts of meaning and purpose—habits that form the inward and invisible infrastructure of democracy."[9] Palmer describes "five habits of the heart": (1) "An understanding that we are all in this together," (2) "An appreciation of the value of 'otherness,'" (3) "An ability to hold tension in life-giving ways," (4) "A sense of personal voice and agency," (5) "A capacity to create community."[10] These habits are assumed in the famous words of Abraham Lincoln, "This nation,

8. Williams, *Open Space of Democracy*, 83–84.
9. Palmer, *Healing the Heart of Democracy*, 24.
10. Palmer, *Healing the Heart of Democracy*, 24.

under God, shall have a new birth of freedom—and that government of the people, by the people, for the people, shall not perish from the earth."[11]

These habits are not possible without their being underpinned by the particular lens of "consensus" or "consent" as discussed earlier. Through consensus, the renewed "habits of the heart" gradually bring together diverse groups of people into a coherent peoplehood according to the vision of those leaders in the founding days of this nation. But again, this is an aspirational, and in some ways optimistic, process. They formed people together into family, church, and townships. Perhaps reflecting the Puritan heritage, particularly as exemplified in the Westminster and Savoy Confessions of faith.[12] The "habits" expressed in these confessions point to the importance of private property, free enterprise, hard work, resourcefulness, and ingenuity. These habits emerged out of the dominant tradition of optimism about our history. In the words of Jon Meacham, these habits are known as "the soul of America."[13] But this "soul" has not adequately acknowledged the fundamental contradictions in our founding that have led to our brokenheartedness. Meacham goes on to ask of these habits: will they defeat the forces of anger, intolerance, and extremism? "There is, in fact, no struggle more important, and none nobler, than the one we wage in the service of those better angels who, however besieged, are always ready for battle."[14] Meacham has a grand but incomplete vision. To round out his analysis I am suggesting that our "better angels" will need to reveal a communal consent to our brokenness if we are to move into a future any different from our past. Are we ready for a change from our history that has not been pretty?

"Consent" is the engine that drives unpretty representational democracy. Yet, as Jean-Jacques Rousseau reminded us, consent takes on the moral and spiritual foundation of civil religion for a society. Consent can be a form of glue to bring people together when its robust meaning informed by a "lived" history is shared by all. In this way consent can provide a kind of sacred authority because of its confessional nature. It allows

11. Lincoln, "Gettysburg Address."

12. The Westminster Confession of Faith is a Reformed confession of faith. Originally drafted in the 1646 Westminster Assembly as the confession of the Church of England. It is regarded as a premier confession within the Presbyterian church worldwide. The Savoy Confession of 1661 attempted to revise the liturgical expression of faith, the Book of Common Prayer.

13. Meacham, *Soul of America*, 8.

14. Meacham, *Soul of America*, 272.

the heart-wrenching reality of our broken, unpretty history to be revealed. Consent is the basic expression of relationship-building. It acknowledges the existence of counter-habits of the heart.

The history of our relationships in opposition is likely here to stay for the foreseeable future. It is not realistic to expect a non-dualistic complementary relationship to emerge in our peoplehood anytime soon. At the same time, Robert Bellah reminds us that our understandings of individual and society are not necessarily a zero-sum situation. In fact, he says "a strong group that respects individual differences will strengthen autonomy as well as solidarity; that it is not in groups but in isolation that people are most apt to be homogenized."[15] The dignity of each individual that Tocqueville calls "equality of conditions" is held in the soul of America. And, individual differences can strengthen autonomy as well as solidarity, though this equality is wistful for some. Which is where an enhanced understanding of "consent" becomes critical.

Solidarity emerges from individual differences in the form of "consent." Consent involves an "equality of conditions" we together uphold that shapes laws, policies, and the ways government functions. The variety of differing views and opinions that emerge in democracy derive from this equality of conditions. Cornel West puts it this way:

> "In this sense, democracy is more a verb than a noun—it is more a dynamic striving and collective movement than a static order or stationary status quo. Democracy is not a system of governance as we tend to think of it, but a cultural way of being."[16]

In other words, West is talking about democracy as more than an idea of the head, but a living history of the heart. Our current separation of head from heart is a clear reason why the alienation of one community from another, and our current phenomena of hyperpolarization, is so alarming. Our "cultural way of being" is threatening the possibility of an alternative relational foundation for our peoplehood. It also prevents the cultivation of a nonsingular consciousness that is so necessary for a future together. Even though it is a complex and arduous undertaking, multiple consciousness is an alternative to our enslavement to the "separate and unequal" way of being that the Kerner Commission predicted.

15. Bellah, *Habits of the Heart*, 307.

16. West, *Democracy Matters*, 68.

We return to the question of this book: What can hold our people together in the society of historical contradictions where we have become estranged one from another and long for just relationship? Our task is daunting indeed. The answer is not at all known nor guaranteed. We the people can endeavor to trust what is at stake for the realization of peoplehood as stated in the preamble of our Constitution. We can do this by interrogating our many layered meanings and cull from them a renewed "living history" that can become shared by us all. We begin with the validity of what was said long ago in this document, but not completely owned for its implications. We do so because the words in the Constitution are what we continue to affirm to be the foundation of our peoplehood. When owned for its deep meanings it still holds today and will hold us together in the future. This is a hopeful affirmation—not an optimistic hope, but rather a defiant hope. Whether these words are indeed the most appropriate basis of our society, we will never know. But these are what we have. We have become what we are and belong to our land in living out these words. Our becoming and belonging of peoplehood are rooted in these words. Becoming and belonging are what we call the soul of America today. Our challenge in this increasingly fragmented and polarized public life is how to discover a new way of approaching and talking about who we really are. This challenge is not a goal-oriented task, it is a journey that we will not cease exploring and one to which we must "consent." Redeeming the soul of America is a consent-driven endeavor and a language-learning journey.

However, our soul rests not just in these words of the Constitution. Our soul lives in the web of people where these words are embodied. They represent both our communal longings for our future and a reminder of our failure to live up to what is said. Regardless of our political views and positions about who we are as people, I believe internally, in our lived life, we do long for relationships that are civil and life-giving. As a people of contradictions, we still hold collective yearnings for the realization of the words of our foundings. And on some level, there is the nagging pain of not being able to live up to these words. Whether we acknowledge it or not, we live out our "internal history," the history of the heart. We are a people "becoming and belonging" in the web of contradictory endeavors, full of kindness and smeared by cruelty at the same time. But we must not give up. Our soul includes a passion that is hope against hope for a better future, a better peoplehood. At the same time, our current soul is not really a place where we feel at home even in our own home. Our restless soul is where we constantly seek becoming and belonging.

IN THE BROKENNESS OF OUR WEB REDEEMING THE SOUL OF AMERICA HAS BEGUN

The peoplehood of contradictions is not something we can erase. We have lived in the state of contradictions for too long. It is not realistic to expect this pattern of life to be eradicated. The primary reason for the continuation of contradictions in our peoplehood is that we have not found a tool that, in the words of H. Richard Niebuhr, "conditions all our thinking and that through this happening we are enabled to apprehend what we are, what we are suffering and doing and what our potentialities are."[17] The "Blessings of Liberty," the epistemological foundation of our peoplehood, is double-edged. It seeks to bring dignity to each person at the same time it makes it extremely hard to see what is taking place in our common web of life. This is the "land of the free, the home of the brave," American exceptionalism. And yet, we continue to relate with each other as strangers as well as neighbors, often treating a neighbor as a stranger.

The "Blessings of Liberty" could complement each other even as they also contradict each other. In our history of race relations this reality has long played out as "Why are Americans so kind and so cruel?" John Lewis lived this life of kindness and cruelty in our broken web. He knew cruelty when he was beaten at the age of twenty-one, when he tried to use a white-only waiting room in Rock Hill, South Carolina. He licked the bitter taste of the soul of America, the brokenness of our web. He knew it again when he was imprisoned at Mississippi State Penitentiary in Sunflower County. More beatings followed. On March 7, 1965, on "Bloody Sunday," Lewis led some 600 marchers across the Edmund Pettus Bridge in Selma, Alabama. The marchers were teargassed and beaten with nightsticks. Lewis's skull was fractured. He bore scars on his head for the rest of his life. He bore the stigma of the broken web of American people on his own body. Was he angry? A conventional interpretation says "yes," he was angry. Why shouldn't he be? But he directed his anger to "good trouble," a constructive energy to address the issues of the civil rights movement. An impressive and inspiring story! But I wonder, where were John Lewis's personal demons long buried? If you follow the life of Lewis, what is revealed is his angry and righteous

17. Niebuhr, *Meaning of Revelation*, 101.

words of denunciations on what he believed to be wrong. He was angry throughout his personal and professional life. He did not hide his anger. He was very critical of those whom he considered to be on the wrong side of his views. In this sense he was very oppositional in relating with people, not complementary. He lived in the very familiar epistemological structure of our peoplehood, how we so often relate with each other. In this opposing way of relating with people, he came to know what it means to "secure the Blessings of Liberty to ourselves and our Prosperity."

> Freedom is not a state; it is an act. It is not some enchanted garden perched high on a distant plateau where we can finally sit down and rest. Freedom is the continuous action we all must take, and each generation must do its part to create an even more fair, more just society.[18]

John Lewis was angry. But his anger was expressed over and over again to redeem the soul of America. As he famously said, "Our struggle is a struggle to redeem the soul of America. It is not a struggle that lasts for a few days, a few weeks, a few months, or a few years. It is the struggle of lifetime, more than one lifetime."[19]

What motivated John Lewis to engage in "good trouble"? My intention here is not to answer this question. His motivations must have been multi-faceted. What is so clear, though, is how his lifework has been received by people. When his coffin-laden procession slowly moved across the bridge where he was beaten, that somber scene deeply moved the hearts of people who gathered there, as well as the hearts of those who watched it on the TV screen. What people saw was Lewis's lifework, the legacy of his lived history of his broken heart that he left for American posterity. The scene told what our peoplehood is about, a nation of contradictions, a society that has been and continues to be divided along the lines of privilege, race, wealth, gender, sexuality, and many other forms of difference. What was apparent at the bridge during his funeral procession was that his life spoke to a large group of people who observed it. His life spoke to the hearts of so many. America has been so cruel to so many, in this case to this person of color. But not just to John Lewis. John Lewis's life was a "revelation," that something has happened to our history that conditions all our thinking and that through this happening we are enabled to apprehend who we are, and

18. Lewis, *Across That Bridge*.

19. Lewis, *Across That Bridge*.

what we are suffering. What is otherwise arbitrary and dumb fact becomes related, intelligible, and an eloquent fact through the revelatory event.[20]

America has received something profound through the story of John Lewis and others like him. In these stories we received a kind of restorative justice, that is, dignity in the midst of adversity, and ultimately freedom to live the life of honesty and human worth in the midst of affliction. The life of John Lewis still speaks to the hearts of people. His story connects with the life stories of those who could tell similar stories, and to those who witnessed his life. John Lewis's story helps connect all Americans together as deeply articulated in our founding documents. John Lewis's life story brings "lived history" alive.

SOLIDARITY THROUGH CONSENT: NEW LANGUAGE FOR A NEW JOURNEY

Our peoplehood is a broken web that longs for mending and healing. Are there concrete signs of reweaving in our fragmented world? Theologian Kathryn Reklis says anger "isn't just release from cultural expectations and the falseness of modern life; it forces (us) to confront personal demons and shortcomings long buried. . . . [A]nger is a purifying fire—unbelievably destructive and dangerous, but also revealing, healing, and maybe even containing a kind of grace."[21] Here she is talking about the miniseries *Beef* that depicts America in our age of microaggressions. "Anger is a purifying fire," injurious and healing. Perhaps this also says something about what "good trouble" is about, a purifying fire revealing who we really are, and the contradictions we live in relating with each other.

Anger as a purifying fire has also touched many Japanese Americans who experienced the internment experience and its aftermath. Satsuki Ina is a therapist specializing in institutional trauma and a co-founder and co-chair of Tsuru for Solidarity. It is a project of Japanese American social justice advocates. Her message is "Stop Repeating History." The goal is to

> end detention sites and support frontline immigrant and refugee communities that are being targeted by racist, inhumane immigration policies. We stand on the moral authority of Japanese

20. Niebuhr, *Meaning of Revelation*, 101.

21. Reklis, "Purifying Anger of *Beef*," 95.

> Americans who suffered the atrocities and legacy of U.S. concentration camps during World War II and say, "Stop Repeating History."[22]

This is a forceful statement, fueled by anger over a gross injustice. In this respect, and through her work, Ina is a re-weaver of the broken web of American peoplehood. Born at Tule Lake Concentration Camp, a maximum-security camp for the incarceration of Japanese Americans during World War II, Ina along with others hung thousands of *tsuru,* origami cranes, a symbol of peace, at the recent immigrant detention center in Dilley, Texas. Ina was there "to let the children inside know there were people who cared about what was happening to them."[23] "When we work across communities, this is where we grow our power to be able to change policy and practices designed to oppress people," Ina says.[24] Her anger purified by fire reveals the pain she and other Japanese Americans suffered, and motivates her to affirm the unfulfilled promise to "establish Justice, promote the general Welfare, and secure the Blessings of Liberty to ourselves and our Prosperity." Solidarity and practicing an implicit "consent" to these ideals by living them become a new "living history." Through working across communities and generations her message is "do not repeat history."

Lisa Doi, a Tsuru co-chair based in Chicago, received more than 300 testimonies from Japanese American camp survivors and their descendants urging lawmakers to pass the reparations bill H.R. 40.

> Japanese American support for H.R. 40 makes sense for many reasons, among them a firsthand understanding of why reparations matter. I can only imagine how redress and a presidential apology might have helped make my great-grandfather whole again, restored his sense of dignity and self. After a hard-fought, multigenerational effort that finally gave former camp survivors permission to speak about their losses and grief, President Ronald Reagan signed the Civil Liberties Act in 1988—and my grandparents, who were imprisoned as teenagers, received the formal apology and cash payments that had eluded their parents.[25]

Doi points to the coronavirus pandemic with its rise in hate against Asian Americans and the recent police shootings of black Americans as

22. Satsuki, "Tsuru for Solidarity."
23. Hayman, "Japanese American Activists."
24. Hayman, "Japanese American Activists."
25. Hayman, "Japanese American Activists."

reasons for supporting current reparation movements. She notes, "Radical change might feel more realistic at a time when people have experienced tremendous upheaval in their lives."

Duncan Ryuken Williams, who is the Tsuru project co-chair, points to the need to acknowledge the historical injuries of different racial groups. "Until we solve long-standing fractures and unaddressed racial animus, we can't become whole."[26] Solidarity of Japanese Americans with African Americans for reparations is a way forward for the future, according to Williams. Reparations do not simply mean financial recompense, but also, at the deepest level, how we "address reparations" at the psychic and spiritual levels so hurts can be healed and alleviated.[27] Solidarity then points to bearing the pain of injuries together: "There's a mountain of suffering out there, and we can't address and solve it as one person. We can only repair it collectively and in solidarity and together."[28]

What helps move race relations toward a reawakening of peoplehood? We get encouraged and our faith in people gets restored when we witness the numerous acts of compassion, sacrifice, courage, and bravery, especially when such acts are least expected. These generous acts tell us that oppositional ways of relating need not be the way of peoplehood in the future. They demonstrate that we really do need each other more than we realize. When we reach out to others out of the realization of painful historical deficits, not out of abundance or strength, then the dawn of the rebirth of peoplehood will commence. The soul of America as an expression of the faith in people might begin to dwell in our collective heart. Is this merely an empty wish? I would say this goal is spurred by defiant hope against hope. What is the alternative? We must acknowledge that our historical paradox is that which binds us—"that part that makes it true that no man is an island is the knowledge that in another way every man is an island," as Buechner reminds us. The rebirth of peoplehood depends on how people will embrace this truth. As John Lewis says, "We are one people with one family. We all live in the same house . . . we must find a way to say to people that we must lay down the burden of hate. For hate is too heavy a burden

26. Hayman, "Japanese American Activists." Duncan Williams is the author of *American Sutra: A Story of Faith and Freedom in the Second World War*, a story of religious freedom under the incarceration of Japanese Americans in concentration camps during World War II.

27. Hayman, "Japanese American Activists."

28. Hayman, "Japanese American Activists."

to bear."[29] The pursuit of the interconnectedness of life is a very daunting challenge. Our identities will become less fixed and stable in the pursuit of such a life. Our lives will become nomadic as we lose our sense of feeling at home. While we might long for certainty, we will need to give up our illusion of precision when it comes to race and other people who defy classification. You might say that we will inhabit a shifting spirituality, a spirituality that bears the same nomadic marks of homelessness and imprecision. This will be a spirituality that learns to trust an unknown future that will undergird a renewed and rewoven peoplehood. The nomadic spirituality dares to live with discontents, the discontents that arise from the incongruence between the nomadic shift of racial identities and the persistent rigidity of race perceptions. This is one of the most serious challenges facing the future of peoplehood.[30] In this state of peoplehood our shared home takes an expression of solidarity. We strive not for "a more perfect union" but toward solidarity with our neighbors, bearing their pain and joy together. The future that is ahead of us relies on our consent to practice the language of solidarity together, as we learn to reweave our torn web.

29. Lewis's words quoted by the Erie County Democratic Committee (July 18, 2020).

30. See Wilkerson, *Caste*.

Bibliography

Adams, John. "Letter from John Adams to Abigail Adams." Adams Family Papers, Massachusetts Historical Society, July 3, 1776. http://www.masshist.org/digitaladams.

"Advancing the Health and Wellbeing of Individuals, Organizations, and Communities." Earl E. Bakken Center for Spirituality and Healing, University of Minnesota. https://csh.umn.edu.

Arango, Jorge. "Meaning in Translation: Illusion of Precision." *Proceedings of the 2010 ACM Conference on Designing Interactive Systems.* https://doi.org/10.1145/1858171.1858208.

Alexander, Michelle. *The New Jim Crow: Mass Incarceration in the Age of Colorblindness.* New York: New Press, 2010.

Baldwin, James. *The Fire Next Time.* New York: Vintage, 1962, 1993,

Behar, Ruth. *Translated Women: Crossing the Border with Esperanza's Story.* Boston: Beacon, 2003.

Bellah, Robert N. "Civil Religion in America." *Daedalus: Journal of the American Academy of Arts and Sciences* 96.1 (1967) 1–21.

Bellah, Robert N., et al. *Habits of the Heart: Individualism and Commitment in American Life.* Berkeley: University of California Press, 1985.

Bormann, Ernest. *Force of Fantasy: Restoring the American Dream.* Carbondale: Southern Illinois University Press, 1985.

Bouie, Jamelle. "America Holds onto an Undemocratic Assumption from Its Founding: That Some People Deserve More Power than Others." *The New York Times Magazine*, August 18, 2019.

———. "Down About the Election? There Is a Speech I Want You to Read." *New York Times*, November 23, 2024.

Brubaker, Rogers. "The Uproar Over 'Transracialism." *New York Times*, May 18, 2017.

Buber, Martin. *I and Thou.* Translated by Walter Kaufmann. New York: Charles Scribner's Sons, 1970.

Buechner, Frederick. *The Hungering Dark.* New York: Seabury, 1981.

Bulosan, Carlos. *America Is in the Heart: A Personal History.* Seattle: University of Washington Press, 1973.

Busto, Rudy. *Revealing the Sacred in Asian and Pacific America.* Edited by Jane Iwamura and Paul Spickard. New York: Routledge, 2003.

CBS News. "Elderly Asian Woman Who Fought Off Attack in San Francisco to Donate Nearly $1 Million Dollars in Donations." March 24, 2021. https://www.cbsnews.com/news/xiao-zhen-xie-san-francisco-elderly-asian-woman-donations-gofundme/.

Charles, Mark. "We the People—The Three Most Misunderstood Words in US History." TEDx/YouTube. https.www.youtube.com/watch?v=HOktqY5wY4A.

Clapp, Rodney. *Johnny Cash and the Great American Contradiction: Christianity and the Battle for the Soul of a Nation.* Louisville: Westminster John Knox, 2008.

Cone, James. *The Cross and The Lynching Tree.* Maryknoll, NY: Orbis, 2011.

Damrosch, Leo. *Tocqueville's Discovery of America.* New York: Farrar, Straus & Giroux, 2010.

DeVault, M. L. "Book Review: Behar/'*The Vulnerable Observer.*'" *Contemporary Sociology* 27.1 (1998) 45–47.

Dolezal, Rachel. *In Full Color: Finding My Place in a Black and White World.* Dallas: BenBella, 2017.

Donne, John. *The Complete Poetry and Selected Prose of John Donne.* Edited by Charles M. Coffin et al. New York: Modern Library, 2001.

Dorrien, Gary. "Walter Earl Fluker's Call to Black Church." *The Christian Century,* July 5, 2023. https://www.christiancentury.org/features/walter-earl-fluker-s-call-black-church.

Douglass, Frederick. *Frederick Douglass on Slavery and the Civil War: Selections from His Writings.* Boston: Courier Corporation, 2014.

———. *Frederick Douglass Oration*, delivered in Lincoln Park, Washington, DC, 1876. New York: Frederick Douglass Historical and Cultural League by the Pathway Press, 1962.

———. "An Oration in Memory of Abraham Lincoln, April 14, 1876." Teaching American History. https://teachingamericanhistory.org/document/oration-in-memory-of-abraham-lincoln/.

———. "What to the Slave Is the Fourth of July?" A speech delivered on July 5, 1852 in Rochester, New York. National Museum of African American History and Culture. https://nmaahe.si.edu/explore/stories/nations-story-what-slave-fourth-July.

Dreher, Rod. "Call Me Rosa Parks." *The American Conservative*, June 12, 2015. https://www.theamericanconservative.com/articles/call-me-rosa-parks/.

Du Bois, W. E. B. *The Soul of Black Folk.* New York: Dover, 2016.

Edwards, Jonathan. *Works of Jonathan Edwards*, volume 2, "Portion of the Righteous." Edited by Edward Hickman. Edinburgh: Banner of Truth Trust, 1974.

Eisenhower, Dwight. "God in America: God in the White House, George Washington 1789–1797." *American Experience*, PBS.

Erie County Democratic Committee. Facebook Post. July 18, 2020. https://www.facebook.com/eriecountydemocraticcommittee/posts/10157088590405919/.

Fetters, Ashley. "How Leonard Cohen's 'Hallelujah' Became Everybody's 'Hallelujah.'" *The Atlantic*, December 4, 2012. https://www.theatantic.com/entertainment/archive/2012/12/how-leonard-cohens-hallelujah-became-everybodys-hallelujah/265816/.

"First Great Seal Committee, July–August, 1776." https://www.greatseal.com/committees/firstcomm/index.html.

Friedman, Thomas. "Let's Change Our Motto to 'Out of Many, We.'" *New York Times*, June 9, 2020. https://www.nytimes.com/2020/06/09/opinion/united-states-motto.html.

Gleason, Philip. *American Identity and Americanization.* Cambridge: Harvard Encyclopedia of American Ethnic Groups, 1980.

Goldman, Samuel. *After Nationalism: Being American in an Age of Division.* Philadelphia: University of Pennsylvania Press, 2021.

Goodreads. "White Feminism Quotes." https://www.goodreads.com/quotes/tag/white-feminism.

Hall, Douglas John. *The Cross in Our Context.* Minneapolis: Fortress, 2003.

———. *Lighten Our Darkness: Toward the Indigenous Theology of the Cross*. Louisville: Westminster, 1976.

———. *Thinking the Faith: Christian Theology in a North American Context*. Minneapolis: Augsburg, 1989.

Hannah-Jones, Nikole. "The 1619 Project: A New Origin Story." *New York Times Magazine*, August 18, 2019, 14–93.

Hayman, Mari. "Japanese American Activists Support Black Reparations to Heal Wounds Past and Present." *Huffpost*, May 5, 2021. https://www.huffpost.com/entry/japanese-american-activists-support-black-reparations_n_607f20934b-3c18bc2a6ac9.

J. Hector, St. John de Crevecoeur. *Letters from an American Farmer*. New York: Penguin, 1981.

Hirasuna, Delphine. *The Art of Gaman: Arts and Crafts from the Japanese American Internment Camps 1942–1946*. Berkeley: Ten Speed, 2005.

hooks, bell. *All About Love: New Visions*. New York: William Morrow, 2018.

Horvat, John II. "Where are America's Habits of the Heart? *Crisis Magazine*, August 7, 2017. https://ww.crisismagazine.com/2017/where-are-americas-habits-of-the-heart.

Hughes, Langston. *The Collected Poems of Langston Hughes*. New York: Alfred A. Knopf, 1994.

Kaplan, Joshua. "Political Theory: The Classic Texts and their Continuing Relevance." *The Modern Scholar*, 2005. Audio lecture series.

Kendi, Ibram X. *Stamped from the Beginning: The Definitive History of Racist Idea*. New York: Bold Type, 2016.

Kerner Commission. *Report of the National Advisory Commission on Civil Disorders*. Washington, DC: U.S. Government Printing Office, 1968.

Kim, Eun Kyung. "Rachel Dolezal Breaks Her Silence on TODAY: I Identify as Black." *NBC TODAY Show*, June 16, 2015.

King, Martin Luther, Jr. "I Have a Dream." https://www.npr.org/2010/01/18/122701268/i-have-a-dream-speech-in-its-entirety.

———. "I've Been to the Mountaintop." https://www.youtube.com/watch?v=gC6qxf3b3FI.

———. *The Papers of Martin Luther King, Jr.* Vol. VI. Edited by Clayborne Carson. Berkeley: University of California Press, 2007.

———. Speech Given in King Chapel at Cornell College, Mount Vernon, Iowa, on October 15, 1962.

Kogawa, Joy. *Obasan:* . Boston: David R. Godine, 1982.

Lewis, John. *Across That Bridge: A Vision for Change and the Future of America*. Audio book. New York: Hachette, 2019.

———. "Speech at the Edmund Pettis Bride." C-SPAN, March 1, 2020. https://www.c-span.org/video/?470112-1/john-lewis-selma-alabama-commemoration.

Lincoln, Abraham. "Gettysburg Address." November 19, 1863. Abraham Lincoln Online. https://www.abrahamlincolnonline.org/lincoln/speeches/gettysburg.htm.

Lorde, Audrey. *Sister Outsider: Essays and Speeches*. Berkeley: Crossing, 2007.

Lowe, Lisa, *Immigrant Acts*. Durham, NC: Duke University Press, 1996.

Matsuoka, Fumitaka. *The Color of Faith*. Cleveland, OH: United Church, 1998.

McDermott, Gerald. *One Holy and Happy Society: The Public Theology of Jonathan Edwards*. University Park: Penn State University Press, 1992.

Meacham, Jon. *The Soul of America: The Battle for Our Better Angels*. New York: Random House, 2018.

Michell, Louis. *Jonathan Edwards and the Experience of Beauty.* Eugene, OR: Wipf & Stock, 2016.

The New York Times. "What Happened in Ferguson." August 15, 2015. https://www.nytimes.com/interactive/2014/08/13/us/ferguson-missouri-town-under-siege-after-police-shooting.html.

Niebuhr, H. Richard. *The Meaning of Revelation.* New York: Macmillan, 1941.

Niebuhr, Reinhold. *Children of Light and Children of Darkness.* New York: Scribner's, 1949.

———. *Faith and History.* New York: Charles Scribner's Sons, 1959.

———. *An Interpretation of Christian Ethics.* New York: Harper & Brothers, 1935.

———. *The Irony of American History.* Chicago: University of Chicago Press, 2008.

Okihiro, Gary. "Is Yellow Black or White?" In *Asian Americans: Experiences and Perspectives,* edited by Timothy P. Fong and Larry H. Shinagawa, 45–68. Upper Saddle River, NJ: Prentice Hall, 2000.

Omi, Michael, and Howard Winant. *Racial Formation in the United States: From the 1960s to the 1990s.* New York: Routledge, 1994.

Palmer, Parker J. *Healing the Heart of Democracy: The Courage to Create a Politics Worthy of the Human Spirit.* San Francisco: Jossey Bass, 2011.

Perez-Pena, Richard. "Black or White? Woman's Story Stirs Up a Furor." *New York Times,* June 12, 2015. https://www.nytimes.com/2015/06/12/us/black-or-whaite-womans-story-stirs-up-a-furor.html.

Peters, Maquita. "Being Black in America." National Public Radio, June 5, 2020. https://www.npr.org/2020/06/05/867060621/being-black-in-america-we-have-a-place-in-this-world-too.

Rakove, Jack N. *Beginnings of National Politics: An Interpretive History of the Continental Congress.* Baltimore: Johns Hopkins University Press, 2019.

Reichek, Morton A. "Elie Wiesel: Out of the Night. *Present Tense,* vol. 3, no. 3 (Spring 1976) 41–47.

Reklis, Kathryn. "The purifying anger of *Beef.*" *The Christian Century*, July 2023. https://www.christiancentury.or/screen-time-beef.

Report of the National Advisory Commission of Civil Disorders: Summary of Report. New York: Bantam, 1968.

Rosen, Jeffrey, et al. "The Constitution, Elections, and Democracy." October 10, 2023. Event video, Hauenstein Center for Presidential Studies at Grand Valley State University. https://www.youtube.com/watch?v=MiJXAmOFlQU.

Rupp, Gordon. *The Righteousness of God: Luther Studies.* London: Hodder and Stoughton, 1953.

Said, Edward. *Exile: Reflections on Exile and Other Essays.* Cambridge: Harvard University Press, 2002.

Satsuki, Ina. "Tsuru for Solidarity." https://www.satsukiina.com.

Sayers, Devon M. "Statue of Late Civil Rights Icon John Lewis Will be Erected in His Congressional District Where a Confederate Monument Once Stood." CNN, December 30, 2022. https://www.cnn.com/2022/12/30/us/john-lewis-tribute-monument-basil-watson-decatur.

Sigrid, Solbakk Raabe. "Strangers." Track 2 on *Sucker Punch.* London: Island Records, 2019.

Slater, Rodney E. "July Fourth: Frederick Douglass FoundHope in the Declaration of Independence. So Can We." *USA Today,* July 4, 2020. https://www.usatoday.com/story/opinion/voices/2020/07/04/july-fourth-frederick-douglass-independence-day-perfect-union-column/5361907002/.

Smith, Archie, Jr. *The Relational Self: Ethics and Therapy from a Black Church Perspective.* Nashville: Abingdon, 1982.

Schneiders, Sandra M. *Theology and Spirituality: Strangers, Rivals, or Partners?* Cambridge: Cambridge University Press, 1986.

Tang, Amy. *Joy Luck Club,* New York: Putnam, 1989.

Thornton, Sharon. *Broken Yet Beloved.* Indianapolis: Chalice, 2002.

———. "Honoring Rising Voices: Pastoral Theology as Emancipatory Practice." *Journal of Pastoral Theology* 12.1 (2002) 45–60.

Tocqueville, Alexis de. *Democracy in America.* Edited by Eduardo Nolla. Chicago: University of Chicago Press, 2002.

Tuvel, Rebecca. "In Defense of Transracialism." *Hypatia* 32.2 (Spring 2017) 263–78.

Tysons. TEDx, "The Truth Behind 'We the People—The Three Most Misunderstood Words in U.S. History." TEDx Legacy, ted.com.

U. S. Decennial Census Measurement of Race and Ethnicity Across the Decades: 1790–2020. https://www.census.gov/data-tools/deo-race-decennial-history/.

USAFACTS.org. "Our Changing Population: United States." https://usafacts.org/data/topics/people-society/population-and-demographics/our-changing-population/.

———. "What Does the Census Mean by 'Some Other Race'?" https://usafacts.org/articles/what-does-the-census-mean-by-some-other-race/.

Van Allen, Rodger, ed. *American Religious Values and the Future of America.* Philadelphia: Fortress, 1978.

Wakamatsu, Peter. "Origins of the 442nd Regimental Combat Team." *Journal of Military History* 58.3 (1994) 45–67.

Seiler, Zoe. "Atlanta Artist Selected To Create John Lewis Monument For Decatur Square." Decaturish, December 30, 2022. https://www.decaturish.com/news/decatur/atlanta-artist-selected-to-create-john-lewis-monument-for-decatur-square/article_371ddfdb-dbdc-55ce-858c-25466d4fd3cb.html.

Webster, Dorothy. "Rachel Dolezal, in Center of Storm, Is Defiant: 'I Identify as Black.'" *New York Times,* June 16, 2015. https://www.nytimes.com/2015/06/16/us/rachel-dolezal-northwest-advocate-identity.html.

West, Cornel. *Democracy Matters: Winning the Fight Against Imperialism.* New York: Penguin, 2005.

Wilkerson, Isabel. *Caste: The Origin of Discontents.* New York: Random House, 2020.

Williams, Duncan Ryuken. *American Sutra: A Story of Faith and Freedom in the Second World War.* Cambridge: Belknap/Harvard University Press, 2019.

Williams, Terry Tempest. *The Open Space of Democracy.* Eugene, OR: Wipf and Stock, 2010.

Wirt, William. *The Life and Character of Patrick Henry.* Philadelphia: James Webster, 1817.

www.ingramcontent.com/pod-product-compliance
Lightning Source LLC
LaVergne TN
LVHW090524110826
845146LV00003B/965